PLENT
FAK
SCAMMERS,
LIARS
AND ME

Please leave a review
on Amazon or fb under the
book title.

Shaan
x

Published under licence by Brown Dog Books and
The Self-Publishing Partnership Ltd, 10b Greenway Farm, Bath Rd, Wick,
nr. Bath BS30 5RL

www.selfpublishingpartnership.co.uk

ISBN printed book: 978-1-83952-335-9
ISBN e-book: 978-1-83952-336-6

Cover design by Kevin Rylands
Internal design by Andrew Easton

Printed and bound in the UK

This book is printed on FSC certified paper

PLENTY OF FAKES, SCAMMERS, LIARS AND ME

The Online Dating Experiences No One Talks About

SHARON J REAH

BROWN DOG BOOKS

Disclaimer

The contents written in my dating memoirs are as accurate as I could make them. No exaggerations of any nature included. The names of those I've dated have been changed to protect their identity.

References to mental health are made and are not intended to offend anyone. References towards abusive behaviour inclusive.

Profanity warning.

I have a strong stomach for most things, but if you don't like the use of swearing but you want to read on, I advise you kindly turn off your filter and embrace my journey. The use of swearing is part and parcel of what occurs in everyday life, and let's be honest who doesn't 'eff and Jeff' on the daily.

Contents

Introduction

Dear reader, it's been forever on my bucket list to share with you some of my most personal moments of my dating journey, by writing my very own memoir experiences. A compilation of dating memoirs that I very much consider as being mind boggling, some filled with heartache, tears, and occasional giggles.

I don't class myself as anything special and I don't particularly feel especially talented. What I do know, regarding the experiences I've had and the choices I've made, have led me into some hellish thunder and lightning moments. Metaphorically speaking, this enabled me to walk through those harsh storms each time, fiercely patting off the lightning smoke. I've chosen to draw my inner strength and balance from those poignant experiences to still move forward.

They say there's a book inside of everyone and I strongly agree with that. The hardest part is knowing where to start. The easiest answer is the beginning. Where is the beginning for me? The Year 2012 is where my dating memoirs began, when I was 46 years of age. Having been single for a while and consumedly busy with a full-time demanding job, three sons and two cats, my social life had halted. The only way to try and build myself a life and find a partner would be by joining the online dating crowd. That's exactly what I did, what an eye opener! I won't apologise for being honestly raw so please kick back and enjoy Plenty of Fakes, Scammers, Liars and Me.

Acknowledgements

W & S: *Thank you for the gift of Writers & Artists Yearbook 2021, because of you both, this book guided me into the capable hands of The Self-Publishing Partnership.*

C & B: *Thank you for the FaceTime chats we had regarding the writing and planning of my book.*

J & N: *Through the recent tears, fears and doubts I've had you've both stood by my side supporting me. I can't thank you both enough.*

D M: *A sister I never thought would be back in my life. Thank you for your verbal support at times when I almost gave up on life and writing.*

D R: *Left us far too young aged 9 years, but you'll always be remembered with love.*

J F: *You and I have known each other almost two years and in that short time it feels like twenty. We've worked through our family disputes, strongly standing united with each other, thank you.*

L McG: *You have always believed in me, even going as far as saying you want me to be Prime Minister! That never fails to give me a laugh. Thank you for believing I could do this.*

M H: *Both of us are alpha, we don't always see eye to eye, but what matters most is the fact we have stood by each other no matter what, thank you for your continuous loyalty. Although no longer living in the same country we both know we are only a mouse click away from each other.*

B C: *After reading a snippet of my dating memoirs, I thank you for your enthusiasm for wanting to buy a copy once published. I hope to not keep you waiting too long.*

L Mck: *A valued friend I miss in my life regardless of our priorities and differences. You always wanted me to write that book and now here it is! Thank you for once being there!*

M T: *Your wise words of comfort supported me through some awful health issues. I'm certain sharing our life tales together helped us grow a mutual respect. You are gone but definitely not forgotten! Thank you for being my genuine friend for the four years we knew each other.*

The Self-Publishing Partnership: *A huge thank you to the whole team for guiding me through my book journey.*

Hungry for Love Not Just a Ham & Cheese Toasty

March 2020 arrived, and it was announced the entire world was plagued by a new pandemic, its name Covid-19. I have lost count of how many health issues I've had to manage over the years, in and out of hospitals having had several surgeries. Now it must be me time, having to be so cautious not to catch this deadly virus. Luckily living in lockdown hasn't changed my life but has changed my thoughts on wanting to be with someone and making a life.

It's about time I had the experience of owning that precious feeling of real love, trust, and friendship. I want it to come banging on my door before the Grim Reaper does. Either he will or Covid-19 will jump ahead of the game.

Most of my so-called friends have dwindled away because of their own life and love bubble. This was before lockdown became a thing. Seems like they don't have time to entertain a disabled singleton! Yeah, huge double whammy. I understand that friendships outgrow each other and sometimes break down but in my situation the ghosting began when I became disabled, and no longer was my own social planner, accepting invites to go out.

Unfortunately, I've come to realise that most of my friends I thought were real friends, painfully weren't. Naturally, that hurts me a great deal. It's like having lived swamped in lies for decades. The realisation of my disabilities hit me hard over and over, I often pointlessly relapse back in time. Becoming stuck in how I was and not how I am or could be. It was then I had a life. I didn't merely exist, and now wondering as I write, where did the last 10–15 years of my life go?

While I dare cast a light of hope in finding that special partner, I need to stop doubt creeping back in. My mind flips back into thinking do I have enough energy to put into a relationship? Questioning myself over and over, will I meet another abuser in disguise? Surely, I can't be that unlucky?

Underneath my sensitive shell, I feel I do want the glimmer, the sparkle that well paired couples seem to ooze. But where is it … the invisible ingredient of love? I know it does exist but finding it for myself is something else. I've seen the 'je ne sais quoi' in family and friends' relationships, extending generally to the people around me too. Up until now I've not experienced it personally.

Being a singleton for years, has me looked upon as if I'm missing something. People look at me as if I'm expected to be part of a couple. I'm a freak because I live man free. I've even had people question whether if I'm gay, having gone so long without having any sort of relationship.

Finally, it's taken me a decade to put pen to paper, can you believe it? All these months in lockdown and the years before that, really have motivated me into thinking about what I want from life, and it's no longer wanting to comfort eat that ham and cheese toasty!

2021 & Still Not Following the Crowd

As a personal rule to self, I don't like to follow the crowd as they say, for several reasons. Gradually I'm learning to stop allowing my erroneous past experiences of men cloud my present-day judgement of moving on. I'm trying to keep that all important hope in finding my best friend.

Observations have shown me that some people purely can't live the single life and tend to move on quickly. From what my own personal experiences have taught me, it's usually for hugely different reasons. I often wonder why so many females, not all, choose to be dependent on men. I'm not being biased, I'm aware it applies to both genders. Men have been known to rely financially on women too.

Curiously though, I'd love to understand more about how most females and males function in a partnership or a marriage as opposed to still being single. I'm not a psychologist or health professional aiming to get a figure for a survey. I'm just saying that for me, I'm constantly asking myself what I am doing wrong. I'd like to learn new things as well as share. I question how people in a relationship make it look so easy. What's the secret? Is there a secret or is everything just a show?

From what I've seen, many people appear to just move on from one relationship to another. Without an obvious glitch or a second thought. As easy as spreading butter on toast and I don't get that. My break-ups have always been bad, so as a result I've found it hard to move on. I get stuck in immense guilt and I'm not always sure why I do this to myself.

Being quite a sensitive soul, a typical Cancerian right from the heart, I love deeply and truly which has on reflection, held me at a disadvantage. To me once scorned is a hard lesson learned. Plus, I do struggle to let down my extensively high barrier once I've been hurt. Once hurt I find it difficult to easily move on, in that respect I don't follow the crowd by jumping vastly into another relationship.

In my head I've held on to what goodness I've had with that person, trying at the same time to blank out the bad. I know I can't simply wipe away my good or bad memories, that's not how my mind functions.

Over the years I've had men depending on me emotionally and financially. Defiantly, I now refuse to ever be in a situation again where financially I'm bled dry. By the time I turned 50 years of age in 2016 I thought I'd be paired with my Swan. Unfortunately, that didn't happen. At my present age of almost 55, I'd love to know how it feels, being able to comfortably depend on a partner. Never did I think I'd become a lonely and isolated woman at my age. Cruelly, life can take anyone down pathways they would never expect to go.

I've noticed that people in the public eye seem the most notorious for moving on. You can't always believe what the media put out there, but you do see many actresses, actors, musicians etc. who don't last awfully long together. Regardless, the majority appear to move on and find happiness once again, quickly. They don't tend to remain stuck on their earlier relationship. Is this their mindset or is it because of fresh opportunities surrounding them?

In fact, it tends to make headline news when a relationship of such powerful dynamics succeeds. When it does succeed it's a pleasure to see. One of my favourite iconic couples are Kurt Russell and Goldie Hawn. Still to this day they look so happy and content with each other. That is the invisible magic I'm talking about. Together they appear to emit naturally as a dedicated couple.

No Man's Land

Some of you readers may relate to how I'm feeling at this time in my life. It's like I'm in constant limbo, no man's land. I know there are good guys out there. However, I still have moments where I struggle to deal with the past, mainly concerning some of the spurious times I've had in male company over the years.

My thoughts swing back and forth like a clock pendulum, trying to convince myself to drop the negativity and remain positive. Yes, thinking more positively, and trying to push past the engulfing negativity that eats away inside my subconscious mind. Sadly, I keep questioning myself about my own failed relationships. Then I ponder on where I've gone wrong and how presently at the age of 55 there's not a man in sight.

I'm the sort of woman that must really think things through and not rush into anything anymore. Maybe this is partially why I can't move on as easily as those who do. Why do I feel overwhelming guilt when my thoughts wander back over the years? It's like I'm trapped within my own past misery. I really need to bring my mojo back!

As I'm getting older and my health isn't like it used to be, it's now time that I do find a partner. Not only for love and friendship but I don't want my three sons having the burden of me holding them back in their lives. I don't want their life choices rotating around me. Neither do I want to grow old, lonely and 'Waiting for God'. But I don't want to settle either. I'm sure this resonates with you too.

Procrastination

Back in 2003, I once joined a dating site, it requested I paid a yearly subscription, so I did. It was the biggest load of freaking crap on the market. All my matches were American. Imagine how frustrated I was at not being able to get a refund back then, never mind a fucking match! Probably due to the lack of available customer service agents. Now I won't pay again unless I'm guaranteed my money back if no success.

While the year was getting underway the start of something began lurking in my mind. This niggle of an idea to share my life's experiences, concerning the difficulties involved in online dating. Thinking to myself, how many readers go through what I've gone through in life, but no one talks about it. Up until now I hadn't made any effort to seek out any dating site. I admit to procrastinating, holding back for several more months. Before I blinked, I realised we were now well into the wettest summer of 2012.

For those of you who haven't used online dating but are thinking about it, I'm hoping you enjoy reading what my experiences have been like. I suppose you could use it to your advantage, like an information tool. Forewarned is forearmed and how true this is. I wish someone had warned me. Why? Because not all relationships have the fairy tale ending, as I personally found out, and not just once. Be great if they did though, wouldn't it?

Becoming a Member in 2012

Can you believe I've finally completed the one thing I never thought I'd see myself doing again? Becoming a member of what seems to be the most popular free dating site in the UK! My hopes are high. I'm in a positive frame of mind and I'm keen to see what this site has to offer me.

In case you don't know most dating sites have a similar process. A procedure where you sign up with an email address and give yourself a username. I decided to go with the unforgettable 'Catfish17'. Considering the dating site had a remarkably similar theme. (On saying that, Catfishing was not my intention, just a fun name I'd chosen added to my lucky number.) Following was a series of questions to fill out my profile. Once this was done, I could then be matched up with my imaginary dream man.

Discovering as I went along, the site joining procedure allows members to skip some particularly important parts. Managing to type in the basics first, I was a bit naughty and took advantage of this. I jumped in and skipped ahead to get started on viewing the male profiles. Always time to go back and add more.

At one point I almost backed out with anxiety getting the better of me. I didn't want to suddenly become deflated in my expectations but decided to carry on with my search. It's the only way to find my match.

After all I am a newbie at this online dating malarkey and it's probably normal to have second thoughts.

Suddenly out of nowhere, I get another wave of doubt creeping back into my already sceptical mind. This simplistic enrolment protocol concerns me. If I can skip ahead and miss out important information anyone can. I don't know whom or what I'm going to encounter, I firmly need to keep my wits about me because it feels like I'm going into battle!

Here I go, I'm all set and have found a few of my best posing pictures. Some of my head and shoulders only, but some full length too. Eek! I thought I looked quite sassy and felt confident enough to upload my pictures. In fact, at this point I was quite proud of my profile, looking as healthy as I could be and feeling great.

My First Online Dating Search

I'm at home and on a day off work, today is the day my real search begins I tell myself. Life is too short to be lonely I say firmly out loud to myself. I retrieve my laptop from under a pile of useless unread letters plonked on the end of my Indian Jali dining table. I plug it in and turn it on. Dancing my fingers across the keyboard, tapping in my password. Hesitantly, but excitedly logging into my account. My heart felt like it was performing somersaults and about to thump its way out of my chest. My eyes almost falling onto my blood red, rosy cheeks.

Within minutes of me logging in I was bombarded with messages. My whole body was trembling with nerves. Feeling like a kid at Christmas being so excited to see who wanted a date with me. Slowly I opened each message one by one. Sighing heavily then whispering under my breath, 'what a bloody mixed bag alright', then my gut began telling me to close the account pronto.

You're wondering why. Some messages were from men who wanted fun. There were men that wanted a fling. Men that wanted a MILF (for those of you readers that aren't familiar with the term it means Mummy I'd like to fuck), yes quite the thing these days. To top it all off, there were men who wanted a cuckolding partner! I didn't know what this was until I did an internet search. Turns out to be a fetish involving a couple.

Often one watches while the other is having sex with another person. Each to their own but not for me.

Oh, the list was endless and so far, I wasn't overly impressed, so I logged out feeling quite disappointed and deflated to be brutally honest. Turned off all notifications on my phone. Unsure of what action to take currently. If in doubt do nowt! That's exactly what I did, nowt. Tomorrow is another day, let's see how I feel then.

Frequently I tend to burn my Angel candle and incense sticks, helping me clear away negative vibes that build up during the day. I love closing my night down burning my favourite Lavender. Watching the mesmerising smoke gliding gracefully through the air spreading its aromatic presence. Creating the relaxed atmosphere, I desperately crave. Gently winding all my senses down ready for sleep. My tired head sinks into my pillow, soon I'm soundly drifting off. Dreaming for some male normality to grab my attention tomorrow. I'm 46 years old, with abusive men gravitating towards me each time I try to date, that isn't tempting at all.

The Tussles of Feeling Good & Bad About Me

Woke up with my head banging. Here comes the migraine along with yesterday's disappointment flooding back into my mind, and no wonder.

I'm quite naive at this online dating malarkey. Only ever had meaningful relationships prior to this in my life and a few non intimate coffee dates. I think I need to find my patience and bide my time for Mr Right. Wholeheartedly, I underestimated how long this full process would take. To try and find my best friend, my soulmate and my partner for life. Unrealistically, I admit, I expected an instant miracle.

The day turned into night, and I simply couldn't face logging back into my dating account. Shattered from work and making sure my boys were fed and watered, I collapsed onto my spacious king size bed. Sliding underneath my freshly changed duvet as I tugged it up to my chin. Within minutes I started snoring like a dilapidated sow but feeling snuggled like a baby.

About the subject of snoring, it's another one of those taboo subjects that women don't like to admit they do. It's either when us ladies are in a relationship or just starting one it becomes a phenomenon. Yes, a bloody phenomenon, because the moment you are told 'bloody hell love your snoring is bad'. Most ladies respond modestly with 'really I didn't know I snored', obviously playing dumb! I'm surmising this is where real love comes into play, when things like snoring are tolerated by either party.

For me I cringe at the thought of me lying there vulnerable. Smudged mascara, hair resembling Worzel Gummidge, and tongue lopped out to one side of my mouth. Feeding saliva in a steady stream onto the makeup-stained cotton pillow. In my head I want to look like Jennifer Lopez but in reality, I look like Lesley from the TV show *Benidorm*.

This is where my insecurities creep in. Being brought up to feel utterly useless, ugly and to hide my human flaws because men don't want to know you have them. I'm happy to say times have moved on since I was a kid. Still, it's such a pity all the negative experiences come to the front of my mind via various triggers, smells or actions. Most likely at this time in my life they won't disappear. To be honest I don't think I want them to, after having gone through what I have and survived. Yes, I'm a survivor, even if a silent one.

Dating Begins

There was never a day I walked into my job feeling like I didn't want to be there. For the first time in my life, I found a career path knowing I was making a prominent difference in many people's lives.

On finishing work and going home I'd make sure boys had their evening meal and homework done. Once they'd gone to bed, I'd log onto my dating profile to see if there were any messages or new matches. To my surprise there were quite a few.

One caught my eye and so I decided to reply to Rusul. Before I knew it, I had my first date set up, planned on my day off from work. In one sense I felt sick, and the other a mixture of nervousness and excitement. I really didn't need to rush out and buy new clothes as I'd been gradually buying things as my body was brilliantly shrinking down.

Now the dating begins, planned on a weekday lunchtime with my decision to meet in a local pub close to where I live. If any issues arose, I could make a quick getaway in my car. Safety always comes first.

We both arrive at the front of the pub doors. I park up as he gets out of a car that someone else is driving. I'm watching as he gets out and on first impressions, he's quite tall, but also not in the best of shape. Anyone remember Mr Blobby?

His picture online must have been from his twenties since he had hair. Presently, he was shaven almost bald. A look I'm not overly keen on to be honest, but it's the person not the hair I'm interested in.

Rusul greets me with a handshake and peck on each cheek. Polite at least, I thought to myself. On closer inspection his clothes weren't really that great, shabby, and worn looking and he wasn't wearing any cologne. For me cologne is necessary, especially on a first date.

We chose a corner table. I sat down as he went to the bar to order me a coffee. He returned from the bar and popped his wallet on the table. I swear real moths had been chewing it. The leather was so worn and bashed it looked ready for the bin. Not a great impression, and I was a bit confused as to why he didn't order anything for himself.

We had a general chat for around an hour then forcefully he tried to kiss me, which I denied. I just couldn't believe how forward this guy was. He didn't take my breath away, he shocked me with his pushiness. As the conversation unfolded it turned out he was younger than me and had diverse cultural beliefs. It was at that point I knew we could be nothing more than friends and he agreed.

He had continued to keep in touch via text and we had a few phone calls which were pleasant enough. Politely he asked if I'd have another coffee with him, just as friends. Not sure why I agreed, possibly loneliness, anyhow we met up at the same local pub again. His manner was quite curt, cold, and even more pushy. It felt like I was with another person. The atmosphere was arguably uneasy. Not feeling comfortable, I thought it best I leave.

He followed me out to my car and grabbed the door handle of the passenger side. Pulling angrily with the intention of getting in. Thinking quickly, I clambered ahead into my driver's side of the car and managed to get in without him. I don't know how I did it as quickly as I did, but once inside I locked all doors in a heartbeat.

I sat shivering into my cold driver's seat. My adrenaline speedily pumped around my body. Taken aback I sat in silence, trying to make sense of what had just happened. What the fuck, why the hell would anyone behave like that? My goodness, he really made me panic. Sitting still anxiously, I waited for him to drive away.

Allowing a good ten minutes after he left, I took a slightly different route home. After what happened, I felt he may follow me. Thankfully, he didn't, and I arrived home safely albeit a bit shaken.

Decisively blocking him on my dating profile and on my phone didn't deter him from ringing from another number or making up another profile, begging to see me. On one hand, he said he wanted to be with me but on the other, he didn't want a girlfriend. This didn't make any sense but screamed 'fanny rat'. Not only was this guy in some way dangerous, but it was also best I avoided altogether.

Bravely Moving On

How that first experience didn't put me off I don't know. Just as well it didn't as I'm bravely moving on, ending up replying to a lovely message I received from a gorgeous guy named Ervin. Sounds silly but this was the first time I could say love at first sight is real.

The picture was of him walking on the beach in his shorts with a very toned physique. Dark hair and tanned. Just my cup of tea! Thought I hit the jackpot, with him being so gorgeous that is!

The messages between us flowed. Ervin mentioned where he lived which was only ten minutes in a car from mine. After the usual introductions, and a few days of texting, he asked me out and I accepted.

For our date I drove to his, where he greeted me in the car park. We stood and talked for about twenty minutes. It was then we went in his car to grab a coffee in a local Starbucks.

Once again, he was younger than me but would never tell me his exact age. He was in shape and into the gym and wrestling. When he revealed his age as being younger, at once I became stand-offish. However, during our date he told me he was looking for a steady girlfriend and that he wanted to settle down. Made a point of telling me my age was perfect for him and that I was what he was looking for. He knew when he saw me apparently, his words not mine.

I was blown away to be honest but because I was looking for the same thing, I was willing to go ahead. Ervin had three grown daughters from his first arranged marriage to a Kurdish woman. Divorced her, and apparently had to pay a huge dowry. His second committed relationship was with an English woman. Similar age to me and he had one daughter with her. They split because she went back to her ex-partner. Bear in mind he told me he had the snip and didn't want any more kids. I felt happy with that because I didn't want more kids either. Happy days and times ahead I thought.

We saw each other a few times before he was able to book a Saturday off work to take me to town for a drink. In town he had two drinks and he was away with the fairies, because he hadn't eaten anything. We flagged down a taxi and went back to his, where he insisted on food. Being sober and feeling like a babysitter I drove us to a local takeaway for a curry.

Once back at his, I just picked at the curry. Having the gastric band fitted meant I had to be so careful with what I ate. Most foods got stuck and I would end up violently throwing up. I tried desperately not to do this on my date as it is a huge embarrassment, but no, I played musical toilets for about an hour.

I stayed over that night and talked while he sobered up. We chatted for hours which felt natural. It felt like we'd known each other for years. Feeding me his various tales, he began to talk about how he'd been a bit of a lad. Sued the police at one time and was trying to have a better life without doing harmful stuff. The stories he told me that night I really didn't know how to take, but the more he was telling me the more he drew me in.

I'd been single for four years at this point, so this for me this was a bit of a thrill … a bit of excitement. We saw each other when he could get the time off work. He was a local chef working late nights for his uncle. So, I accepted that some of his time was taken up with seeing his daughters and weird work patterns. Plus, I worked demanding shifts and had my boys to prioritise.

The more I saw him the more he told me about him being involved with drugs. I didn't like this! The way he'd suddenly disappear then come back gave me huge doses of anxiety. He had my head absolutely minced. One night he put a ring on my finger, yes third finger, left hand and asked me to wait and be patient for him sorting his life out. Suddenly, out of the blue, I'd get abusive texts followed by apologies. I can honestly say I fell in love with this guy not sure why, but I did. Until one day I'd had enough, and my love turned into almost hate.

As I was driving along to his flat with his ring and some things, he'd bought me, I was planning on what I needed to say to end it all. Knocking and tapping on his door, no answer came, but I felt he was home. Leaving the ring and gifts he gave me in a cheap plastic carrier bag balanced on his front door handle. No note was attached but I remember it being teatime on 31st of December 2012. What a way to end the year but it had to be done as devastated and disappointed as I felt.

2012 merged into 2013 and I heard nothing from him for months, then he emailed me to contact him, so I did.

Needing some sort of closure, I was curious how he just seemed to disappear off the planet. I needed an explanation. He'd told me he'd given up his rented council flat and moved to the north of Durham. Now he was settled, he wanted me to drive down and see him. Being so unexpected I was taken aback and refused to just drop everything.

Then the volcano erupted, a whole load of abuse spewed out of his mouth and down the phone. When I put the phone down, he sent awful texts. I responded calmly and kept myself composed. But what he didn't know was that I was in pieces, crying, my blurry eyes even more red and inflamed.

That night it was meant to be the end. I wanted no further contact. I didn't need him bringing me down and expecting me to jump to his every whim. He unleashed the controlling, abusive, narcissistic, and untrustworthy part of him I didn't fully see before.

My gut kept telling me this wasn't right. No one deserves to be treated this way. He really broke my heart. This time I had to dust myself down and start again. Why bloody why did I fall for him? I really wished I hadn't.

I thought the best way to get this guy out of my head was to get back onto the online dating scene and move on.

Wanted Mr Right but Met Mr Camp

It wasn't long before I was approached online by a guy who seemed like the total opposite of what I'd usually go for. Thinking opposites attract, what possibly could I lose!

He'd not long come out of a marriage, starting a bitter divorce, I thought hmmm let's see. Chatting casually about his background, which was quite grand compared to mine, I thought why not go on a date with this David and then decide.

We met in town for coffee where he brought me a very unusual gift! He suggested we go to a local art gallery restaurant where we'd have lunch. I thought that was a posh suggestion, so off we went. As we arrived the head waiter greeted us. 'Hello, sir, I see you're back again'. To my horror David replied, 'Oh yes I'm doing a spot or two of dating this week'. How embarrassed I was, hole in the ground swallow me up quickly!

The staff had sectioned off a part of the dining area especially for us, which was amazing. However, the immediate killer as I'm sure all you readers would agree, was the comment referring to his multiple dating. Can you believe he told me he'd done the same thing for each of his dates that week?

We had the meal, then a stroll around the art gallery. All I could think about was 'I'm on a freaking crappy date get me out of here!'.

How I remained polite throughout my gritted teeth is a mystery. Time was getting on, so he gave me a lift back to my car. When he pulled up, I just wanted to jump out and say bye, but he kept me talking and put me on the spot for another date. How could I say no to his face? Yes, I know I'm a coward.

Fate worked in my favour as I didn't go on that second date. We spoke a few times after that but agreed to just leave it on friendly terms. I also had given him a little dating advice. 'David,' I said, 'Do not bring a used purple wicker ball as a gift for your date.' Yes, you read correctly, he brought me exactly that. 'Please bring flowers,' I advised seriously, but with sarcasm. His response was, 'Ah but I could replace it with something more expensive in the future.' Presumptuous I thought, we don't have a future!

David shortly after sent me a message proceeding to tell me how he was now dating a professional woman. She'd booked and paid for them a hotel room on the Quayside. I made a comment of at least she's getting more than a washed-out purple wicker ball tonight! Swiftly he told me to piss off. I couldn't help but squeal with laughter. What another lucky escape. Another 'fanny rat' he proved to be. Only this time a posh, chubby camp one!

Hot Chocolate with Marshmallows!

I'd put time between the last awful experiences to try and start again. Looking through my messages, I spotted a guy who had the look of Errol Brown. For you readers who don't know, he was the vocalist of Hot Chocolate. The guy who sang *You Sexy Thing*.

A conversation was struck up between us, quickly merging into regular phone calls. It turns out he was an Irish guy named Jed and of mixed race. Living in the beautiful area of Yorkshire.

I'd explained to him I couldn't go out anywhere as I'd not long had surgery on both feet. We'd spoken every day for a week on the phone. He really was so genuinely caring but there was something I really couldn't fathom.

On the phone I shared with him how unhappy and worried I was about the healing of my feet, the next day he turned up on my doorstep. In his arms were the biggest, most beautiful bouquet of mixed fresh flowers. Now that is the type of gesture I appreciate. I always have said to my boys, 'buy me flowers to enjoy while I'm alive, as I won't have a grave for you all to put them on when I'm gone'.

Over the next week things moved extremely quickly, he kind of swept me off my wired toed platformed feet! Well at least I thought he had and to be honest I was happy to have that happen.

As the weeks progressed, I saw how he was more interested in making my boys happy rather than me. All fair and well but he started to put my boys before me. I just felt like I was at the bottom of the queue for some adult attention.

Jed has one young son Leon who is autistic. He told me he had him quite a lot on most weekends, it was easy to see how much of a great dad he was. I know I sound ungrateful, but I wasn't looking for a dad for my boys. Maybe I was being selfish for wanting someone for me.

The more I got to know Jed, the more I knew something was different in the way he processed information. We were on a totally opposing level. It wasn't long before he started to crush what very few brain cells I had left. Often, he had me demented, I tried to be on his level, but it wasn't working. Most of the time he couldn't grasp things I'd say to him, even when repeated.

One of my previous jobs was working in a school with autistic children. Being autistic, I knew Leon could be challenging. It wasn't long before my sons were introduced to his son. Leon didn't want to speak much even though he could so this wasn't a surprise. Considerately, we all adapted and went along with what made him feel comfortable.

My boys finished their bowling practice at the Alley early Saturday lunchtime. We all headed across to Asda to buy something to make lunch back at home. Nothing could have prepared me for what happened next.

Above the entrance of Asda is a security camera TV screen mirroring you as you walk into the store. We walked casually through, my boys and I behind him and his son. Leon was deeply captivated in watching himself on the security screen. Out of nowhere he decided to jump back to repeat the process of walking in again to see himself on screen.

At that point I yelped like an injured dog! He only managed to jump back on my toe that wasn't healing. I was so angry, while at the same time crying in excruciating pain and frustration.

Both my boys held me up on either side as I hobbled back to my car. You can imagine that didn't go down well at all, even though it was an accident. I did seek an urgent appointment with my consultant, but my toe was so severely damaged he couldn't fix it. My consultant referred me to another hospital, so I had to start the process all over again and have further corrective surgery soon.

The next incident was when Jed picked me up in his car one Saturday afternoon, he wanted me to attend his tattoo appointment with him. Considering the tattoo had something to do with me, I felt compelled to go along.

I've always loved swans and how when they find their mate they stay together for life. For years I've always wanted to have that strong swan bond in a relationship. Though not ever had anyone on the same level as me to want that.

Jed had booked into a tattoo studio to have two swans tattooed on the inside of his wrist. Why? I'd mentioned the swans to him at some point. I did try to talk him out of doing it but that was a waste of time.

We arrived promptly for his appointment, which happened to be upstairs. I found this quite selfish of him, considering he knew of my struggles with my feet and legs. Reaching the top, we were greeted by an older woman who was surprisingly tattoo free on first glimpse. Then there was a younger girl who looked around eighteen years old. You could clearly see her body had an exceptionally good relationship with tattoos and piercings.

We said hello to both staff, and he mentioned his appointment time.

The younger girl noticed that he was drinking a can of American root beer. 'Mmmm,' she said, then in a sultry flirtatious manner said, 'does that taste nice?'. I could not get my head around his fucking response. 'Here take a drink of it'. He handed her his can. She gripped it and took a slurpy gulp while making eye contact with him. I stood there, arms crossed, looking at him then looking at her, feeling invisible. Her arm reached across the front desk and in front of me as she handed it back saying, 'ah that's so nice thanks'. What the fuck was that? You'd think it was the norm to drink out of some strangers can! I was in utter shock as I stared non-stop at him. He stayed silent because he started to get panicky over the pain involved with the tattoo process.

We were in and out in around forty-five minutes. His tattoo where he wanted it was OK. I thought it was a silly place to put it but hey-ho, not my body or my choice. His gesture was extremely sweet as he wanted the swans to replicate us, so I kept my opinion to myself. He did tell me that his intentions with me were long-term involving marriage, but I couldn't see that happening, ever!

As we walked back down the staircase of the tattooists, I couldn't wait to see what he had to say about sharing his can of root beer. I asked him calmly, but I'm sure he could see in my face the expression of disgust. He honestly looked puzzled and didn't have any clue why I was disgusted. At that point I offered him my advice. 'The next time you offer a girl you don't know a slurp of your root beer, think about where her mouth has been the night before'.

Suddenly his face went from a smile to a bloody big perplexed frozen glare, the penny dropped, and he finally grasped my point. All these things he did or said were building up in me, to the point I was giving myself horrible migraines as well as losing patience.

When I would think of his actions, I'd suddenly have outbursts of hysteria and laughing. Things would just hit me. I'd then think how I would cope long term if I can't cope short term? This human being clearly needs constant guidance and explanations every day. It was like having a child's mind in a man's body and this made me physically sick, drained and ill. Times when I was near boiling point, and he didn't even realise. He'd just smile. I'd rather have a cup of hot chocolate with marshmallows than go through the agonising mental torture of remaining in a relationship with Jed. Hang on though before you roast me, keep reading.

'Hi Babe!'

This week had flown by. Planning in advance from last week to pop to Aldi Saturday afternoon. Jed and I needed some food and snacks to do something nice for the boys. I was driving, he was in the passenger seat and my two boys were in the back. His phone rang and to my surprise he answered, 'Hi babe'. I didn't know where to look or what to think. Could he have another girlfriend? It crossed my mind! Focusing hard driving over to Aldi, I tried to not make it obvious I was earwigging in on his call.

My interpretation of using the word babe towards someone would be if you're in a relationship with them. Or say, for example, you have girlfriends or even boyfriends and use it as a term of endearment. The South of England seems to use this more loosely than the North from what I've heard.

To my shock horror he finished his call and casually told me it was his sister. I was utterly thrown sideways and thought I was going to bump my car.

Surely, I'm not the only one to think this is weird? Oh no, he insisted I was the one who was thinking wrong. To mainly prove to myself that I wasn't losing the plot, I launched a Facebook survey amongst my family and friends. I asked who thinks calling your sister babe is acceptable. Several people attributed their views resulting in a thread of almost one hundred comments. The majority saying no that's very wrong, except for Sandra and Pete. We have a vastly different view of appropriateness and that is absolutely fine, but I was not going to lose on this one. What I didn't mention on the feed was Jed openly disclosed to anyone who'd listen, that he'd been sexually abused as a child by his aunts. This did put a different angle on things.

I Can't Unsee What I Saw

Picture this, Jed and I had arranged to meet up with two friends of mine, Sandra and Pete. A night for a few drinks and a chat in our local pub. The night had gone reasonably well, and it was time to leave. We all walked towards the porch exit which was decked with heavy smoked glass exit doors. Pete walked in front of me into the car park and straight ahead towards their car, behind me walked Jed and Sandra.

The porch music was drowned out by the echo of a sloppy kissing sound, so I turned around to look. At that point couldn't see anyone kissing only Jed and Sandra both locked in each other's arms hugging, directly looking into each other's eyes. I guess that's bound to happen when both people are only 5ft 1" or thereabouts. However, this is the first time they'd met so seeing that, well let's say I wasn't a happy bunny!

Honestly, I could not believe my eyes. I don't think Pete heard or saw what I saw either. Wow, I was bloody livid. I think you can guess what happened when we both got back to mine. The air was blue!

Things were becoming more and more fraught between us, and the tension was building. I could not understand how his mind functioned at all. Subsequently, I didn't see the point in mentioning anything to Sandra, knowing she'd say it was nothing and I was overreacting.

Maybe it was nothing, but from my point of view it wasn't OK. Not sure how things would have gone down if the shoe were on the other foot that night. This battle was not worth fighting over losing a friend and I knew he'd be history soon enough.

His reason for kissing and hugging her that way, he was just being friendly! Friendly my hairy fat arse! What the fuck and who the fuck goes on like that? I certainly don't, but unfortunately, I can't unsee what I saw!

Fucking Hell, It's Attached!

Jed and I certainly weren't heading in the same direction in life. It dawned on me at that moment that my caring side had kicked in again. Repeatedly I was trying to fix another broken man.

Talking about boiling point, the following weekend he travelled up in the afternoon to see us all. We were chilling in my living room, the two of us comfortably sat on either side of the sofa drinking tea.

The high sun was beating in through the patio doors of my conservatory and rays bounced onto my pale drained cheeks. It was glorious and the silence was just too perfect. So much so you know when something is about to go down. Too right it was, fucking bang on cue!

A thud of a hand planted itself hard on my left cheek. My cup of tea was rested on my chest as I lay tilted back resting on the cushions. Yes, it was him once again, lunging a fucking attack on my face. It was like he was plucking a fucking chicken and it really hurt. My hot mug of tea, I was enjoying, went everywhere except my mouth. My top half was soaked along with the sofa and carpet. Sharply I turned to look his way while hearing the words 'fucking hell it's attached!'.

As it turns out I had an unusually long isolated blonde facial hair. That hair caught his eye on a sunlight beam. He then blithered out, 'oh I thought it was a cat hair'. My cheek was left throbbing like a heartbeat. I really didn't know if I wanted to thank him for spotting it or plank him for saying it. What I did know is that I was feeling smaller than a garden dwarf. Not to mention a hairy bloody ape, I was so embarrassed. Who the fuck does this type of thing?

After he yanked my facial hair out, I calmly put down my cup. Stomping upstairs in a foul mood to tell my two younger sons what had happened, and how I couldn't face Jed.

One of my sons went downstairs and said to him straight out, 'Mam is upset and can't speak now could you leave please'. So, he did. At that moment I felt an immediate relief lift from my heavy head, it was like a miracle.

These feelings I have don't only stem from him but also from my dad. Growing up, maybe around eight years old my dad got up close to my face and said to me, 'you're growing a moustache, you need to shave that off'. I felt so small, ugly, hairy, and so embarrassed. Running upstairs to the bathroom, on tippy toes I stretched up to reach into the bathroom cabinet and take out his Gillette razor. Angrily I took this to my face with the intention of removing every trace of fine blonde hair. Little did I know then about the consequences of facial hair removal. I thought once removed it wouldn't come back and then my dad wouldn't mention it again.

How very wrong I was. I'd started something so unnecessary but at such a youthful age I had no idea what the long-term results would be. It was my dad's actions that day that silently scarred me for life. Where hair was concerned, he gave me such a complex all over my body. Something I still carry with me today but if anyone mentions my body hair, I don't give a shit anymore. This is me, end of, I'm too old to care about trivial issues like that ever again.

Give Flowers and Not a Used Purple Wicker Ball

Having had surgery on both feet at the same time, they had to remain wrapped in thick bandages with wires visibly sticking out of my toes. I was not able to walk much yet, so my friend Libby, suggested we'd go to the Metrocentre. We window-shopped while she was casually pushing me in a wheelchair. She thought getting me out would be a lovely change of scenery, and she was right. We came out of House of Fraser. My stomach flipped. At times, my eyes could be annoyingly blurry. On approach to us I noticed a guy I'd gone on one date with a little while back, David. He was the one who took me for lunch at the art gallery. (Yes, the lunch was free for us because of his connections, he didn't pay a penny. How do I know? He told me!).

Somehow, he ended up changing direction and walked past us. He was accompanied by a young tall slim redhead. She was clutching quite proudly, a large, beautiful bouquet of fresh brightly coloured flowers. Hesitantly, he slightly turned his head to the side, noticing me sat in the wheelchair on passing. Libby and I giggled as we looked at each other, but we kept on moving. Surprisingly, he did a full 360 turn, back over to greet me.

We had a few pleasant words, and as he started to walk back over to his date, I couldn't help but say 'nice flowers' while grinning. He obviously had taken my advice and bought her flowers. Better than giving her a used worn purple wicker ball! All was not lost!

A Blast from the Past

It's only a month away from Christmas 2016 and a blast from the past happened. Remember Jed? How could you forget?! Unexpectedly, he called me wondering if we could be friends because he'd not gotten over me. Me being me said yeah, but not really thinking of the consequences of what I agreed to. In fact, most times, I put others before myself because I don't like hurting anyone's feelings.

I'd arranged at Christmas for the boys to go over to their dads on Christmas Day, at 11.30 am. They don't routinely have Christmas Day dinner, so this was a new experience for them. I wanted to be alone to reflect over the last year and think about what changes I needed to make for the New Year.

Casually over a call I mentioned this to Jed, he suggested he book a lovely table at a restaurant as a surprise. He invited me to chill and be looked after, since I'd never been looked after by a man before. Neither having had a Christmas dinner cooked for me nor even been out for one since leaving home, I fell to temptation. Yeah, I thought, why not end the year on a positive note? I'm so stupid for thinking that!

Christmas Day arrives, and the boys leave promptly for their dad's. Jed turns up looking very dapper and we leave straight away to our surprise destination. The weather was chilly, and ice began to set on the ground from an earlier snowfall. Conversation was pleasant in the car on the way down, halting as we arrived outside a retail park.

My eyes nearly popped out of my head. The fucking 'Hungry Horse Pub Chain' in Yorkshire was his idea of being looked after. Now let me clear this up because I sound like a real spoiled bitch. I enjoy the Hungry Horse Pub Chain for a lunch date, for example, but not to spend Christmas Day there. This was his idea of a lovely restaurant, but it wasn't mine. We clearly still hadn't reached the same wavelength.

We sat at our table for two in the window, picturesquely the snow started to fall as the day became night. The pub was warm and cosy just like you want Christmas to be. Inside me, my anxiety started to gradually build up. Through the glass window we could see the snow was lying on the ground, glistening as if sprinkled with glitter. All I could think about was if I got fucking snowed in with him.

Staff came over to explain how our Christmas dinner was self-service at the carvery station, and to go and help yourself when we were ready. We moseyed on up to join an empty queue. Yes, that's right no queue! We stood by the serving station expecting hot food. Stomachs were growling like starving wolves. I was so hungry my mouth was salivating as I'd not eaten all day, the smell of Christmas dinner was making me drool.

Lovely jubbly, I thought to myself, eagerly I peered over the counter into the stainless-steel serving dishes. Bloody hell, this was not the view I imagined. By the look on my face (if I could see my face) I must have resembled an extremely disappointed hungry banshee.

Nearly everything had gone and what was left was barely warm kitchen scraps. No steam rising above the trays inside the serving station. Common sense should have told me not to get my hopes up.

My stomach sunken like the Titanic, I was ready to go onto the nearest motorway to find a cow, to barbecue there and then, not giving a shit about the snow.

The staff suggested we try something else, so I ordered a lasagne and he ordered fish and chips. Eagerly we waited for nearly an hour for our chosen meals to be served, only now by skeleton staff. Hardly any customers were inside and the snow, just like the lyrics 'snow is falling all around us', was getting heavier and not melting anytime soon. Conversation between us was mediocre. My poor empty growling stomach was going crazy, and I could feel my IBS (irritable bowel syndrome) rumbling in the background. In fact, it had my attention more than the conversation did.

Our meals were finally brought to our cosy table for two and it was at that point my anxiety steadied. I just wanted some piping hot food. I didn't know how to react when my first bite of the lasagne was still frozen. Maintaining my dignity, I stayed pleasant, calm and patient while I waited for my second attempt at lasagne being cooked. That's if they did cook a fresh one instead of reheating the original frozen dish.

Maybe another half hour passed, and it was served, steam belting out of it. I picked up my fork and stabbed firmly into the centre of the lasagne. It looked delicious with the cheese still melting on the top. I couldn't wait to have a full stomach. Taste buds were salivating. The smell was so gorgeous, but then I could have cried. Once again, my lasagne was frozen in the middle.

Jed ate most of his meal but there was no way I was attempting another dish. I didn't want food poisoning and by now I was hangry (hungry and angry), I wanted to leave. Speaking to the management and with a little verbal resistance from them I managed to get Jed a full refund. He'd paid upfront weeks in advance to secure a Christmas booking. What a disappointment for both of us.

Oh well, karma bit my fat arse and hasn't let go since! This was the first time I'd arranged for boys to go to their dads for Christmas dinner. I won't do that again! Probably takes the prime medal for worst Christmas as an adult in my entire life. Why the fuck did I do it?

Human Boomerang

I find myself full circle back to Ervin who ghosted me. As you know he'd continued to send the odd text and email persistently, asking to meet up. I'd play him like I mentioned earlier, occasionally ignoring him or saying OK, then at the last-minute cancelling. Silly games I know but it gave me enough satisfaction to know he can't have what he wants, when he wants. Turning the tables back on him. Considering he previously left without saying a word, I was so hurt not knowing what happened.

Mid-January 2017 and he called me wanting to see me face to face. Very rarely did he do that, so after we talked, I agreed. Things to me never really ended because he just left his rented flat and disappeared without trace. Ultimately, for my own sanity I needed some sort of closure. Naturally, I wanted answers, getting them was another matter. I told him I'd cook us lunch and we'd talk in depth at mine.

The following day after our call he turned up around noon. As I opened the patio doors, he lunged forward at me. Both his hands grabbing both sides of my face and planting the most meaningful long kiss on my lips.

In the moment I froze, I didn't know what hit me. To be honest I didn't know how to react, I was taken aback. Seeing him for the first time in so long, I didn't even know if I fancied him anymore. He looked scruffy, as if he'd been sofa surfing for ages. Wishing I hadn't, I caught a glimpse of his nails, they were long, neglected, and filthy like he'd been digging trenches. My stomach turned in disgust.

We sat down and I asked him if he'd like lunch put out in my conservatory, sitting at my dining table. 'Oh, I don't want lunch, I was at a friend's house last night. He cooked for me, and I couldn't refuse, in my culture it's rude. Today my stomach isn't too good as I ate too much'.

Being very bloody tempted, I wanted to say I've spent time cooking for you, isn't it rude to refuse me? With great difficulty I held my tongue and refrained from saying anything. Although my face must have said it all. To myself I thought you fucking ungrateful, inconsiderate biased monster. Imagine how infuriated I felt. I'd used all my energy to cook, and that was something I was doing less and less of, even for my boys. Then I imagined him eating beside me with those filthy long creepy nails, and thought I'm saved! What a damn turn-off, I had to hide how sickly they made me feel.

His story for my ears followed the lines of working on getting a clean reputation. No longer being involved with the bad boy lifestyle. He certainly didn't give me that impression as something didn't add up here! As a while ago he told me he was living in North Durham and was settled in a privately rented house. He'd now got me curious as to why he'd changed his ways.

He sat leaning forward on my sofa, both elbows resting on his thickset thighs. His head robotically turned, then his shallow brown eyes scanned my living room. It felt like he was waiting for something to happen, having me on tenterhooks set my gut off. Spontaneously, he came out with wanting to move in with me and give things a proper go. He didn't even look me in the face while asking! I was stumped with confusion and felt shocked in the moment. What the fuck is happening? I was thinking to myself.

My mind was shot at the whole scenario, so I gingerly put this to him. 'What guarantee do I have that my boys won't get dragged into your past unhealthy habits?'. You may be thinking why is she bothering to ask him? Previously, he told me 'They' still have his number and even though he's out they keep track of where he is. Thinking to myself, is this guy living in the real world, because he sounds like a right 'Jackanory tell us a fucking story'? To me, realistically he'd been watching too many Liam Neeson films, *Taken* springs to mind!

For the same reason, how could I not consider what he told me? Supposing it was the truth. Highly unlikely, but what was clear to me was that this guy has unresolved mental health issues.

He did compliment me on my looks which was flattering, however I doubted everything that came out of his lying mouth. Inclusive of when he asked to borrow £3k.

After he dropped the bomb, he ranted off plenty of tales, chatting non-stop for two hours, spewing from his mouth like hot volcano lava. One of them was that he'd been to London where his main contacts were based. While there, he'd been driving around the streets in his boss's Lamborghini. Forced at parties to have gorgeous escorts. Do you think *Need for Speed* was another of his fantasy films? It was at that moment he asked to borrow £3k. In my head I was laughing, but my stomach sank rapidly. Thinking to myself do you really think I'm that stupid? With my serious face I asked him why he needed that amount of money. Never was he going to get a penny, but I was wanting him to think he was!

'I owned a car garage that was burned down not long ago. I don't have business insurance because it wasn't a legal business. All my money is tied up back in my home Country. Until I can sneak funds into the UK, I need money on my hands. I only deal in cash, leaving no money trail,' he said, like it was a rehearsed sob story. My response, 'I'm so sorry but I don't have that kind of money'. He tried to be OK about it, but I could see by his body language he was pissed off!

My boys were due back from school, I asked him if he'd like to meet them, again testing his reaction. 'Erm I've got to go, I'm shattered, I need sleep'. I knew he'd say that which is why I asked him on the spot! Naturally, he left with no money from me. As he left, he said, 'love you. I'll text when I'm home, relax and trust me, as now I'm serious about us'. 'Serious my arse,' I mumbled as he was leaving. He has a plan and I'm his tool of some sort!

My heart was still feeling the pinch of what he did in the past to me. My inner thoughts were screaming text him to fuck off. So not twenty mins after he left, I started the 'dear John' text via Messenger. While I was writing it, I received a text from him telling me how serious he was about me. Well, it must have hit him like a shitstorm when he received the text reply telling him I didn't want him back. I then waited for a further reply. Nothing arrived back so before any abusive messages followed, I blocked him.

He must have thought I'd have said yes to taking him back. I've always treated him respectfully and kindly, not this time. My way or join the highway bitch, I said under my breath. It certainly felt great taking back my life.

The Birth of Purple Lavender

Things were settling into 2017 and trying to function as 'normally' as possible so I decided to make up another dating profile and rejoin the same free dating site online. If I remember correctly, I called myself 'Purple Lavender'.

By now my reasons for finding love weren't the same as they were originally. I've now found myself with extremely limited mobility and becoming more in need of support. Fibromyalgia is, on a daily basis, making my muscles become weaker.

Looking ahead I don't want to impede in any way my three sons as previously mentioned. I started to think again, positively telling myself I should have a partner soon. Detesting any thoughts of me ever getting in my sons' way.

The practicality for finding love has changed once again quite dramatically, in just a few years. I'm able to still function and walk a little plus still have mental capacity. I feel scared though, all of it could be taken away from me before I find my soulmate. I've truly never experienced receiving true love, but I have given real love to a select few of the wrong undeserving males. What a waste of my time, affection and life.

Fetish Shocker

Purple Lavender logs into her online dating account to find a pleasant message from a guy who lives in Seahouses, local to where she lives. Michael and I messaged for a day or so and then agreed to meet for coffee.

He was there waiting at the local shopping mall where, greeting each other, I asked him to walk at a slow pace towards the coffee shop. He reciprocated and mentioned he had a crushed kneecap from doing army service and that he couldn't walk fast even if in a fire! The upside of that made me feel a bit more comfortable and I began to warm to his persona. The downside was I didn't fancy him.

In the past I've gone for good looks and yes, they've been total arseholes in one way or another. Now was a different approach I'd adapted, aiming to go with the flow. We arrived at the coffee shop, I sat down, and he didn't hesitate to buy our coffee. The conversation was going quite well so he ordered a second coffee for us. Hmm, I thought I might get a second date here if things keep going smoothly. Hold that thought! He decided to tell me that he had a urine fetish. I didn't dare say I needed the toilet in case he turned out to be a pervert that liked to watch females urinate! I sat cross-legged for at least an hour while I listened to him elaborate.

Quite openly he went on to tell me how he loves a golden shower (being peed on). I'm trying to keep a serious face on while he's talking until, he then blurts out 'Oh I also love a finger up my arse and being spat on'. Trying to take in what he had told me, he then finished with 'I love to spit too, not to mention my cock is pierced'. I excused myself to the toilet where I was peeing for England, at the same time not knowing if I wanted to laugh or cry. Quietly sitting in the toilet cubicle jostling with ideas of how I could fucking get myself out of this awkward conversation!

Hiding the fact, I'm obviously freaked out by his first date fetish shocker! On returning to the table, I politely kept things short and direct. I said, 'thanks for the coffee I need to go now, things to do'. He stood up and said, 'this is awkward what happens next?' I just shook his hand, then he leaned into me and pecked my cheek. We both left to my relief.

After arriving home about fifteen minutes later, my phone pinged. He was asking for a second date. I politely declined saying we weren't on the same sexual level. Recommending that he not disclose anything so personal on a first date in the future. He didn't understand why not, I wasn't about to tell him the ins and outs and punish him like a little boy. I think he'd enjoy it too much! Oh well, another one bites the dust!

First Date & Engagement Ring Shopping

The day darkened into night before I turned around. I can't tell you how I managed to muster the energy to log back into my dating account, it's a miracle, but I did. There awaited a message from a guy based in Stevenage. Extremely keen to get the train up to meet me.

After several online messages and an exchange of many text messages and calls, over a week's duration I agreed. I had butterflies for the first time in ages, I was so excited. Telling my family at the time due to 'stranger danger' ha-ha. Imagine if I didn't return home? I think I'd be slightly missed due to the backlog of laundry!

Date was planned and I was to meet Alex off the train in Newcastle. As the time drew nearer, I started to feel a bit hesitant. My anxiety was nearing 8.4 on my own Richter scale. The older I grow the more I think of how much stress a date can cause! I was attracted to him from the pictures I saw, I guess this time was different because of how he did look.

My son and daughter in law helped me calm down by driving me over to the Central Station. They stayed discreetly in the background like Hercule Poirot and Agatha Christie. Albeit that gave me the confidence to meet Alex and greatly helped calm my obvious anxiety.

Here he comes walking down the platform with a great big grin, waving at me. Looking tall, well-groomed, and handsome, like his actual picture, hooray! We hugged warmly like old friends, but then he went in for a kiss on my lips. I swiftly turned away and said, 'I don't kiss on a first date'. He then jokes 'roll on the second then'. He obviously likes me as we both chuckle.

We began to walk up towards the centre of town heading for The Gate, an indoor food mall. As we were walking, he grabbed my left hand. All I could think about was if I remembered to put my hand cream on. Nothing more uncomfortable to hear, than a man telling you you've got hands like sandpaper. Silly me looked down at my hand holding his, to realise I was wearing my leather gloves.

As we walked and talked, he didn't realise the pain each step was causing me. On a first date I was far too embarrassed to blurt out too much about my health issues. I remained suffering in silence.

We approached some shops, including a string of jewellers on Northumberland Street. Walking at a snail's pace, browsing in the windows. I really didn't know what to say when he'd asked which style engagement ring I'd specifically wear. I just pointed to a style and said, 'that's quite pretty', then asked him why. As he cleared his throat, he confidently said, 'for future reference'.

In one sense I was flattered but in another I was repeating in my head fucking hell what am I doing, it's a first date? Been there done this with the ring scenario and I'm not going there again this early.

We'd stopped for coffee at the top Northumberland Street. He bought the first and I offered to get our second and he accepted. On we went to The Gate and into Frankie & Benny's where we ordered our food and chatted. During the conversation I didn't feel any click, especially when he took off his coat. Unfortunately, he revealed a belly resembling the size of a washing machine drum. The type that manages a heavy 11 kg load. Not generally minding someone on a slightly larger scale, but I wasn't feeling it. The size of his belly was a huge turn-off.

Moving on to the end of our meal, I politely offered to pay for my own and he again accepted. At this point I sort of knew it was not going the way I wanted. I was hoping to be looked after for the first time in my life. On first impressions I don't think this guy was the one to do that.

To finish the night, on the way back in the direction of the station I had asked the two detectives to meet us beside The Mile Castle Pub downtown. As Alex and I approached, there they were, outside, freezing cold waiting for us to go inside.

Introductions to my son and his other half complete, we entered the pub, glad of the heat warming us all up. I couldn't manage the stairs; my legs were far too weakened from the walk. How embarrassing it was for me to have to be taken by staff to the service lift at the back of the pub. It was stacked high, filled with beverages and snacks for the bar. They chose a table, and on looking around I eventually found my way to them.

Alex had asked me to buy a few rounds, so I did without question. I didn't want him thinking I was a sponger for his money. Similarly, I felt like he could have been more generous towards me. Night was closing in, and it was time for his train back. We all accompanied him to the platform where on departure he once again tried to kiss me on the lips. Once again, I said no. He then belly chuckled and said, 'Oh Ok, not in front of the kids'. I didn't really think it was funny, I just wanted to go home and rest as the exhaustion had caught up with me. Alex showed he could talk the talk but not walk the walk!

Heading back home in the car, we all discussed the night. My family thought he had potential until I explained about the window shopping for a ring. This was a red flag immediately to me. My gut was bouncing that sinking feeling around telling me to bail!

On saying that, we did end up having a laugh all around and all enjoyed how things progressed that night. I took our picture with my phone before we left the pub. It turned out to be a nice one, so I sent it on to Alex by his request.

While in the pub, I noticed the environment wasn't too noisy. I was grateful for that, as I can't bear noise anymore. Another awful condition that attaches itself to Fibromyalgia.

The following morning things got off to a weird start. They pretty much ended the same way too. He text me to say he'd booked a local Travelodge near to where I live. Not that I had shown that to him. I gave him an idea of the area only. It was two weeks until Valentine's Day and he was planning on coming up to stay for two days.

He mentioned looking for a new job up North and bringing his 10-year-old with him to live. Everything was on his terms and moving faster than broadband. No discussion with me at all.

Having a habit of testing men in the beginning of getting to know them, I asked him why he hadn't put our picture up on his WhatsApp like I did on mine. He answered saying he'd have to ask his 10-year-old son for permission! Woah, I thought, no way am I being dictated to by a 10-year-old. While on the phone I'd asked him if he'd researched Fibromyalgia like I asked. 'Nah, I've been too busy booking my son and I tickets for the next rugby match this weekend'.

That was the straw that broke the camel's back. If he made time to book tickets, surely, he had the time to do an internet search for an illness. It was especially important to me to know where I stood with him. I explained, and he just didn't get me at all. Politely I ended it and as I did so, all he rambled on about was the hundreds of pounds he'd spent on me.

I was astonished, at a loss at how he'd supposedly spent that amount of money when I paid my own way. Unless he secretly bought me a ring? Still, he thought he could gaslight me, but I'm too long in the tooth to accept such controlling behaviour. On several occasions he continued texting me. The more I ignored him, the more verbally abusive and manipulative he became. No thank you, so I did the sensible thing, and I blocked his number. My new name is now Ms Blocker!

Can Anyone Tie Their Own Shoelaces?

It wasn't long before I received another message from a guy who lived in Newcastle. His picture profile was blank, so I asked him what he was hiding from. 'No one,' he said, then popped on his profile a head and shoulders snap of him. He had tanned skin and was heavy set, mentioning he was self-conscious of his size. His picture didn't reveal his total size, so I had no clue what I was in for.

I managed to gain his trust as we chatted over a few days and then MJ asked to meet for coffee. Immediately I go to my safe place which is Costa Coffee on the High Street. Making my way down in a taxi, I got there on time. Not knowing the best place to wait, I decided to stand inside the foyer of Tesco. Very easily accessible with lots of small businesses set up inside like a small indoor market.

I'm standing still looking around and out the corner of my eye I see MJ spying on me behind a stall. I didn't know if I should giggle or be freaked out, so I pretended to look around and not see him. After about ten minutes he showed his face and waddled towards me, all twenty-five stones of him. I kid you not his knees could barely be seen. Poor soul was struggling, and I could empathise.

Since Costa is only two minutes away from Tesco, we took a slow walk over. Inside we grabbed a seat where he got the coffees in for us. For once I thought to myself thank fuck the attention is not on my walking, the pressure was off me this time and on him!

A pleasant conversation flowed, and he chatted about all the baggage he had. He was of Moroccan nationality living in the UK for quite some years. Splitting with hostility from his English wife. Together they had a young daughter, where he was battling for custody and working as many hours as he could.

Tediously, I felt like his counsellor to be honest, distinctly having the impression he had very few friends. Feeling a bit sorry for him I explained that I was happy to have a friendship but nothing else. The date ended and we went our separate ways.

While waiting for my taxi I received a text within minutes. Full of compliments and that he felt lucky he met me. As a friend could I help him through this tough time? Off the cuff I said yeah, no problem, never thinking he'd call me the next day. On the call he was begging to have another coffee with me to obtain my advice. After I had a few days of rest I met up with him again later in the week.

We both stood at the counter inside of Costa. 'Oh,' he said, 'I've got no change and the credit card machine in Tesco is down'. I ended up getting the drinks in and thought we're even now, I'm in no one's debt!

All he talked about was a woman at work who fancied him, and how his wife was wanting him back. I thought this guy doesn't need my advice. He's so insecure needing to tell me that he is wanted, where instead I thought he needs to give his head a bloody shake and sort himself out. I'm not getting involved in any drama regardless of who it is, it could be Jason Momoa for all I care.

I said I needed to go, made up an excuse and called a taxi home. This guy was in a very confused state looking for a fuck buddy. He had no confidence and just wanted an easy fix to his complicated world that I didn't want to be any part of!

By the size of his waist, I doubt he could manage to tie his own shoelaces, and there was no way I was doing that! Not to mention there was zero chemistry from my side! The texts kept coming and I didn't want any part of it so here was another one I added to my block list.

Confirmation To Self, Height Matters

The week passed quickly as we know time stands still for no one. I logged back online into my dating profile not knowing what to find as choices were becoming slim pickings. This guy didn't waste any time and basically asked straight out 'when am I free for lunch?'

Well, I thought 'way to go' I like that, rather than endless messages back and forth on the site. His picture was quite nice, but his height was described as only 5ft 6. I generally prefer a much taller man but thought there are other things more important to me than height. I crushed those thoughts and decided to go.

My anxiety was still up and down not knowing what to expect. We mutually decided to meet at the Monument, in Newcastle City Centre.

I arrived there about five minutes early and there was no one to be seen. Nervously I kept looking around and checking my phone. Wearing a bright red raincoat, I was hard to be overlooked, then I heard a ping from my phone in my pocket, it was a message from Ronan. It read turn around. Lifting my gaze from my phone in a slow and creeped-out way, I began to turn around. The first thing I heard was a roaring of silly laughter then a face practically nose to nose with mine still laughing. I had to stop myself from automatically screaming. Shock horror, his profile picture must have been from twenty plus years ago. Not only that, but his face resembled an extremely angry ripened clingstone plum, very tanned and heavily wrinkled.

Then we have his height. Why is it that some small men lean towards lying about their height and add on a few extra inches? This one did. Is this what people refer to as little-man syndrome? He must have been all of 5ft 2. I could have coped with 5ft 6, but those four inches make the world of difference to me. I don't want to feel like I'm with a child or want a man looking up my nostrils.

I honestly felt like we were a couple of Oompa Loompas on a day out from the Chocolate Factory. I had my false tan on, I'm not very tall, I'm wearing red and walking with a waddle, bloody hell I couldn't even make this one up. It's safe to say there was no immediate spark from me, but there would have been sparks coming from my shoes if my legs were capable of running!

In all fairness this guy was very polite and did ask me where I wanted to go for lunch. I let him decide, we ended up going into Chiquito's, which was newly opened at the time. We were shown to our table promptly.

As we sat down before I even got the chance to exhale and shake off my anxiety, he asked me what I wanted to drink. I didn't want anything alcoholic, but he insisted I had a large margarita. He chose something else in the form of a cocktail for himself. I would have been more than happy with my usual one-shot latte.

Drinks came along and I took my time with nano sips, I had no plans on being tipsy, or paralytic! Not sure what Ronan had in mind, but he wasn't tagging on home with me. I got the impression he could be a bit of a leech, by the way he walked so close beside me, invading my space. Mind you on saying that it could have easily been my cross-eyed waddle clashing into his space.

Not many customers were about, and our food was served extremely quickly. He kept saying to me, 'order another drink everything is on me it's my treat'. As generous as that sounds I wasn't about to take advantage of his wallet that's just not me. Immediately I knew there was no chemistry so why would I use him.

Trying to enjoy my lunch he just didn't shut up. I couldn't say the conversation flowed because it wasn't from my side. Having the impression, he really liked me, meant I couldn't really sit there like a cardboard cutout, so I vocally contributed with the odd ok or nod.

That progressed with me trying to engage by asking him some general questions to pass the time. Beginning with how he became single, by heck that was complicated.

He settled here many years ago as an immigrant on his own and then met his ex. She had several kids, but she split up with the kids' dad when they were all little. When Ronan met her, he brought them up as his own. When they split up, he remained in touch and was referred to as Dad and Grandad by them all. He never married but wanted to marry her, but she didn't want another marriage.

Changing the direction of his chat, he mentioned he could no longer work due to health reasons. He described back pain and poor walking issues. I didn't judge even though I'd observed him get up and down from the table, going to the toilet quite a few times. Mind you by this time he'd quite a few different alcoholic drinks that could have numbed his pain. In general, he didn't seem to struggle to walk which I thought to myself was a bit strange.

On one occasion when Ronan came back from the toilet, he started talking about how he claims full whack on all government benefits. Gets a free bus pass to travel and is out on lunches or dating quite a bit trying to make friends as well as finding a girlfriend. He boldly told me he doesn't worry about money. Why? Back home in his own country (his words not mine) he holds many properties that were on derelict land. He said he could sell but was waiting for the right time to do so. I asked if he had declared all this to the UK government. He exaggerated 'Noooo', the government are thick here, they never check up!

He was cheekily mock laughing as he was telling me this. I was raging inside knowing the real mental and physical struggles I've had in my life, on top of how hard it is to get the right benefits put in place when needed. It was something I knew from experience of supporting the clients in my last job too!

Our main meal was finished, and he began slurring his words. Being of very slight build, the alcohol had clearly gone to his head. The effect gave him a continually loose tongue. We were sitting waiting for our dessert when he began talking about another recent dating experience.

'A blonde good-looking lady got in touch with me on the dating site. We arranged to meet up for a drink on a night-time in a pub near both of us. We'd had a few and it was almost closing time. By heck she could fucking drink that one,' he said. 'She called a taxi to share, but it ended up with me getting out at hers as she kept hinting, she wanted sex. I thought I'd oblige.'

As he's telling me I couldn't help but laugh at the whole situation. 'We didn't mess about, she led me upstairs to her bedroom. At first, I thought ewwww it fucking stinks up here, so I asked her where the toilet is. She points to the bathroom across the landing. I tried to be quicker but I'm away for about five minutes washing my hands and cock.

'Walking back into the bedroom I'm ready for business. She's lying on the bed slightly propped up waiting for me to climb in, patting the pillow saying hurry the fuck up. As I'm stripping off, I'm still smelling this fucking awful stink. I'm down to my T-shirt and underpants and I had to mention the smell to her. It was getting stronger as I got closer to her bed. I lifted my leg to climb in as she simultaneously pulled back the duvet. It was as if she was cracking a fucking whip, only to reveal the biggest shit I've ever seen. While smiling she said, 'I have a shit fetish climb in'. I halted in motion as I was almost on the bed, speechlessly I fell backwards, landing hard on the dirty carpeted floor. 'No fucking way', I said, grabbed my clothes and left. He finished off telling me she told him, she made it before she left for the date ready for him coming back with her!

I just can't get my head around some people's desires, it invades too much of my mind space thinking about it. At that point I didn't know if I wanted to laugh, vomit, or have a meltdown because he was so serious! He didn't find it funny, and I could see by his expressions he was in shock about the whole experience.

The bill was brought to the table, and he checked it. Then he gave it to me to check. He insisted on paying even though I tried to pay my way, but he was adamant he was paying. As we walked towards the exit of Eldon Square all he went on about was how much the meal cost. He thought he was robbed even though it was checked twice. I thanked him and offered once again to pay my way. He refused but still seemed perplexed over the cost.

We departed going our own way and within minutes my phone pinged asking me out again. I politely declined and I thought that would have been that. Oh no, a string of drunken voicemails and messages bombarded my phone over a day or two. They'd gone on to say how I've deserted him, used him for the meal, and that I'm missing out on a good man. For fuck's sake what a drama queen, he's delirious!

Trying hard to stay calm and not stress wasn't working. Why should any woman have to have these emotionally manipulative and abusive texts, so initially I ignored him. A few weeks passed and, on several occasions, he made up other dating profiles and sent me abusive messages. I just kept on blocking him, since he left me no choice but to do so. At the same time, I remained polite and kept my dignity which probably fired him up more. Instead of feeling relief I feel so much guilt every time I block one of these broken men because I know they need support not a date!

This online dating is unbelievably hard work and if anything, causing my anxiety to rocket, I feel like I want to scream hysterically, wouldn't be the first time and certainly won't be the last. In fact, my usual let off steam trick is to clang a few kitchen cupboard doors while having a yell to get out my frustration! My sons will say it's Mam and her singing cupboard time! You should try it, it's very therapeutic!

Ken Didn't Meet Barbie

April arrived and for years it's been the shittiest month for me, so here I am again logging into my dating profile, yawn. I replied to a head and shoulders picture and a very polite message. Dark hair and dark beard with glasses. His height being described as 5 ft 9 and of large build. I wasn't sure how large he was so the only way to find out was to meet him on that coffee date invite.

Tuesday late morning and I'm in a taxi down to my local safe place Costa on the High Street to meet Ken. He was already sitting at a table for two but stood up quickly to greet me then to the service counter to get me a latte. I noticed he still had his heavy winter coat on.

Conversation was a slow burner but then he started to share openly about matters concerning his almost finished divorce, telling me his soon-to-be ex-wife was of an Asian background and her links were to some sort of big worldwide gang. At this point I took things with a pinch of salt because I'd already had so many 'Jackanory Tales' from previous dates, I thought it best to avoid any in-depth chat about those topics. Changing the chat direction, a little, he talked about his several lines of work and his young child.

After our first coffee Ken removed his coat then stood up from the table to visit the loo. As he slowly pushed himself up from the table his belly sprung out and did a kind of bounce just like Jessica Rabbit's boobies! I pretended I didn't see because I was so embarrassed at how large he turned out to be.

Ken must have been around twenty-three stone and only 5 ft 8. His shirt must have been 5X. I'm no Barbie but I'm not in 5XL size clothes either. However, the positive thing about Ken was that he had manners, the old-fashioned sort and that's what made me accept a second date.

Sunday arrived, and so did our second date day, where Ken previously offered to take me for a meal. My son was at work that day, so he drove us both to the Metrocentre, where I found a coffee shop and sat until it was time to meet Ken.

Ultimately, he would have noticed how bad I am on my feet, so when we met up, I explained about my poor mobility. We headed into Nando's close by.

I'm not sure why on dates I choose saucy sloppy food because I mainly miss my mouth at a high percentage and decorate my clothes. You guessed it, I managed to stain my lovely new blouse. He laughed at the greasy dark stain on the front, but I felt awkward and tried to pretend it didn't happen, I didn't know what else to do. At that point I changed conversation and offered to pay, his response was 'You get the next meal'.

We talked a bit more, when he slipped into the conversation him having one close female friend Jess. I may sound suspicious because in general I am. I started to wonder how close he was with this woman because the last thing I want is trouble. He told me she was helping him clear his home of junk. 'Junk,' I said, 'what kind?' … 'oh, failed business goods, bargains I've picked up along the way and to be honest I can't throw anything out,' he confidently replied. I was shocked further when he told me she was clearing a safe space to get into the property. I'm assuming planning ahead for me to visit!

Fucking hell, was my silent immediate thought, this guy is a hoarder. Just like the ones seen on TV. He eats for comfort and has obviously not recovered from his ongoing divorce situation. Or maybe there was more to it that I didn't know about.

Time ticked on and my son met me to take me home. I said bye to Ken, and we left. Something wasn't sitting right in my gut, so I had to text him to say that I felt we weren't right for each other. He then blocked me, obviously being pissed off that he didn't meet his Barbie. I wasn't judging his mental health but what I didn't have the time, energy, or effort for was supporting another broken man. I could not allow myself to be in that position once again.

Did I Hear Right?

A week or so passed and I felt ready to log back into the dating site to retrieve any messages. To my surprise my inbox was full, no it wasn't, it held one message.

This guy was around 45 years old with no hair and a tad bit of dark stubble and glasses which isn't what I like but thought he was worth a date. We exchanged a few messages between us and then Adrian asked me out.

He wasn't overly tall, 5 ft 10 in his profile and was on the larger side of what I generally like, he must have weighed at least eighteen stone. With my past experiences how can I trust a profile or picture, it's a potluck blind date each time?

Struggling to get myself dressed, I managed to get a lift down on to the High Street to meet at the local Costa. As stated earlier, a place I know familiar faces and feel extremely safe to be. Having the other advantage of not being too far to walk from a nearby taxi rank either. Reassurance to myself, that I didn't need to feel embarrassed about Adrian having to see me walk too much. Arriving nervously at the top of the indoor lifts in Tesco, with Costa only a stone's throw away.

Adrian arrived five minutes after me, appearing at the top of the escalator, greeting me with a sombre look. At once I knew there wasn't any physical attraction on my behalf but didn't want to be rude and leave.

He was very polite, but I got the impression very, very selfish and a guy that pretty much wasn't the type to compromise on anything. Yes, all this from first impressions but hang on before you judge me. I didn't dismiss him because there wasn't any spark as I've heard people say they've grown to love someone's personality. I told myself to just be patient and see.

During the coffee date a client I once supported was sitting at a table behind us and approached me, accompanied by her Support Worker Emma. She walked over to say hi before leaving, giving me a bit of a jump as I hadn't seen her sitting behind me.

The situation perplexed me to be honest, because not one member of staff from that same company bothered to contact me to see how I was doing. Very strange to not receive any leaving best wishes or gifts which is the norm. To then this sudden 'hello' situation! On thinking a client would not be encouraged by staff to speak to an ex-employee either.

Anyhow, I reciprocated and indulged in a little conversation. Emma started to chat away like old times at work taking Adrian and myself by surprise. As she giggled, she mentioned she was pregnant with a baby girl. Conversation still focusing on Emma, she then mentioned how she was looking forward to having a baby sister for her son.

Casually I said congratulations, following on remarking on how I was pleased she was finally settled, as prior to this she was a single parent enjoying her nights out with flings along the way. 'No,' she immaturely giggled, replying, 'I had a one-night stand with my son's dad, it just seems like we are matched for having babies, but we can't be together.' I was dumbstruck, so was Adrian by the look on his face. After she left, he said, 'did I just hear right?'. Then we laughed in dismay shaking our heads in sync. I was thinking about what has become of youth in society today, choosing to 'breed' without any fatherly commitments. Here's me, wishing I had had that commitment from the boys' dad back in my time. However, I respect her decision to choose that way of life.

The date ended and we went our separate ways. That was that no second date, no text, no nothing. Oh well, nothing lost except my confidence, as I started to feel sorry for myself. Paranoid thoughts about how I walk and how I look crept in. But I know I must try and shake them off, it's easier said than done though.

The Return of the Human Boomerang

Thursday 27th of June arrived, another ordinary day, I thought, until I couldn't believe my blurry vision as I opened my Messenger chat.

I couldn't sleep and the first thing that many of us do when we wake up is check our mobile phone. At 03:16 am early hours, a message was waiting for me simply saying 'Hi'. It was from Ervin. Not feeling impressed I went back to sleep but wondered what this piece of shit was up to. However, in all honesty I was expecting a message I just didn't know how long he'd take.

When I woke up later that morning, I decided to play a little game. Especially since I knew he was playing with me. How do I know that? you'll be saying to yourself. Well before I answered him back, I checked out his open Facebook profile. Probably before he realised, I was back in his Messenger contacts. So what? you readers may say! I sound like Frank Carson the comedian 'and there's more'. This is the explanation of what happened before he sent me the 'hi' as like I said, I was expecting contact. He is so bang on predictable.

Two days prior to him getting in touch, for some reason he'd popped into my mind. You know when you revisit the past and you dwell a bit on things, well that happens to me a lot, especially when there's unfinished business. My mind doesn't settle.

Now you've all snooped on Facebook, don't deny it. For me to snoop I had to unblock the shit. Once unblocked he showed up on my Messenger chat and I would have been on his, you know the drill.

His Facebook had a picture of him and a female in quite a snug pose and to be fair she seemed like a person that I would get along with. I looked through what pictures I could, and it appeared that he'd been with her for at least a year. She was also a professional older woman, that I was told looked a bit like me. Yes, I screenshot a picture and asked some family and friends what they'd thought, I had to. At first, I tortured myself a bit because he would never take a photo of us, saying he hated his picture taken. After that I never pushed him for one as he'd get agitated. I'd finished snooping and just waited. Tick bloody tock. Two days later came the contact.

After our chat I checked out his profile picture. He'd changed it for a picture of two little girls that looked absolutely nothing alike. His status was now single and so was hers. I knew the face of the older girl she was his daughter, he had pictures in most rooms of his flat. The second girl I could only assume was his too.

During the chat I didn't know he had a second daughter, so I asked him about her. He told me he split from his ex after he met me in 2012. Originally, he told me he was single and had the snip, I was fucking livid he'd pursued me in 2012 on a dating site. Ever so convincing he wanted a relationship with me and no one else. He was with me at the time he was still seeing his ex and she got pregnant at some point. Basically, he lied to me and lied to her.

I managed to stay calm and polite knowing it was the only way to get my answers and possible closure from the time when he ghosted me. However, he quickly ended the chat when I asked about Consett and then said I now live there. I told a little lie, as I don't live there or want this lowlife sniffing around my real address. My aim was to have him panic at the mention of that area. I was the one in control now not him. He deserved a bit of cat and mouse.

Now the reason I said Consett was deliberate because I noticed his most recent ex-girlfriend lives there. Her Facebook page was transparent, and in my opinion, she posts far too much on there! He must have shit himself, thinking fuck both exes living within minutes of each other. Far too close for comfort, I can't shag around there, they might know each other. That's how he ticks concerning females. The chat ended for now, but I knew there was more to come, and I was ready!

Games Nothing but Games

Soon the 13th of July came around, not sure why but I had an uneasy feeling. I just knew something felt off but didn't know what. As I was browsing my Facebook posts something just made me think about Ervin. I'd not bothered to look at his Facebook since he contacted me in June. I was trying to block him out of any thoughts to be honest, and I was getting better at it.

There it was the evidence of just how much a lowlife 'fanny rat' this creep was. It was his girlfriend's birthday, they had gotten back together, got engaged and were flying away to Egypt. All within a space of three weeks of him last being in touch and asking to see me.

Games nothing but games with this player. It was so easy to find this information, as like I said earlier, anyone can see what's going on in her life she posts every little thing. I'd noticed he'd changed his profile picture back to him and her and his status to engaged.

My thoughts weren't of jealousy or anger, they were for this poor woman, I knew he couldn't be faithful to her or anyone for that matter. At this point I was so tempted to get in touch with her to warn her about him, but then I thought, no it's not my business. She'll have to find out the hard way like I did. He'd taken up too much of my headspace, seven years of it, I'm not allowing him more.

The Rucksack Saga

Now early September and we're on the last few months of 2019. For a few years I hadn't made time to start a fresh look on the dating site, so I logged back into my profile and refreshed a few pictures of my updated poses, none with the ridiculous trout pout look though, I just can't be doing with filters or that pathetic crap.

A University Lecturer had gotten in touch and at first, I thought he was a scammer, but as it turned out he was just terrible at asking females out. However, after about three weeks of chatting Noah managed to ask me out, I thought why not? He's very polite, not smaller than me, not bad looking and he seems ultra-keen.

The coffee date was planned in Costa in Newcastle City Centre. It was situated just up from my bus stop, ideally chosen so I wouldn't have to walk far. Purposely avoiding embarrassing myself with how poorly I walk.

Arriving early, I sat drinking my latte by the window waiting for him to arrive, people-watching at the same time. Taking a sip of my warm milky froth, I glanced to my right-side view, there was Noah. Unbelievably and practically running speedily as if competing in a marathon, I had to do a double take as he whizzed on by.

Carried on his back was a huge rucksack bag, almost larger than him, bouncing around in all directions. I had to contain my laugh as when his head turned right to look into Costa, his worried brown eyes greeted my curious blue ones. I half lifted my left hand hesitantly waving at him, hiding my laugh. His whole body came to an abrupt halt, then in military style he about turned to go find the entrance. I thought, what the fuck? It was so hard holding back my childish giggles.

Noah found the entrance and approached me like he was still competing in a race. While in front of me he gave little eye contact and at the same time he said, 'hey', then sat down in a fluster, removing his huge backpack. The most important thing I noticed was that he wasn't totally like his picture. One of the first things he said to me was, 'I'm losing my hair do you mind a bald man?' Simultaneously, he took his hand and patted his longer strands of black hair. Discreetly trying to place them back on the top of his balding head. Then flicked them back with his fingers like he was some sort of Adonis. I wanted to laugh again because his whole energy felt comical but not all in a funny way, it was strange. My stomach sank with a retching feeling, thinking oh no this is another replica of Jed!

He sat with no drink and after a short while finally offered me a coffee. As he made the offer, he continued with, 'I can afford to buy you at least a coffee as I'm self-funded. Oh, and I'm not after a Visa either I have a card to show you I'm a university student!' After him saying that, I couldn't help but decline, it just felt weirdly wrong like I was sponging from him.

Previously, I was under the impression he was working at the University but no, he was in his final year of study and around ten plus years younger than he'd said he was online in his profile. Oh, my days, this is all wrong!

During our chat he disclosed to me that if I became his girlfriend, there would be no touching or kissing. He was profoundly saving himself for marriage being a staunch virgin. 'I'm a mug get me fucking out of here'. I really wanted to shout those words so loudly from Costa's doorway, but instead I said calmly to Noah, 'I have to go now for my bus'. 'Oh, I'll come with you to the bus stop,' he said. For fuck's sake, he's insistent!

We joined a queue as we stood together at the bus stop. I noticed he was staring at my hair. 'What colour is your hair now because it looks like a mixture of blue, blonde and grey?', he asked. 'Yeah, well done, that's exactly the colour it is,' I sarcastically replied. Why on earth did he have to mention the grey?! I thought to myself, no woman likes her grey roots mentioned, he's very inexperienced with what or not to share with a woman. Then he started asking me why I didn't colour my hair completely blonde. My response was, I like it the way it is, no one else has hair like mine so this is me!

He waved me away on the bus, like a toddler does a wave to its mother. I sat feeling panicked, not being used to going anywhere alone, never mind getting on a bus. Then the panic attack started affecting my breathing, while I was focusing on my breath it hit me, what the fuck just happened?

It took me months to eventually get through to this guy, that he wasn't for me, but we could remain friends. It certainly became clear that being friends could not continue. Then he started pestering me by asking if I had any single friends available, this made it crystal clear he was searching for some female to intimately practise on. There was absolutely no indication this guy wanted a serious relationship. At that point I learned I had to be more vigilant, while being more wary of liars on the dating site. They'll say anything just to get your knickers off, I've experienced that first-hand.

A Businessman & His Jalopy

Next in touch, a businessman from Bradford who'd settled in Newcastle. Mick asked to take me for a meal, so I chose somewhere local to me.

That was where I felt comfortable, and I knew my sons or my daughter in law could be on standby. More so if I needed any one of them to make a quick escape It's an advantage to be surrounded by family with cars, I wasn't stuck for choices.

On saying that, I took a taxi down to the local pub, where he pulled up at the same time as me. After bragging on the phone to me about his fleet of posh cars, he turned up in what seemed to be a clapped-out work van. My thoughts went straight to Del Boy from *Only Fools and Horses*. Fucking hell here we go again, I thought to myself.

He stepped out from his jalopy in work gear continuing to chat on his phone. By this time, I was out of my taxi and standing waiting for him to walk over. I was looking at him, waiting for him to make eye contact while greeting me. He didn't end his call or really look too far up from the ground. I thought what a cheeky, bad-mannered git. Feeling very tempted to leave but I thought that would be a waste of my taxi money, I may as well stay for lunch.

At last, he tilts his head sideward and up while half grinning at me on his approach, as some sort of indication he acknowledged I was there. I turned around and walked ahead into the pub reception, from there, we were escorted to our reserved table. As I turned around to see if he was following me, he was, but still on that bloody call. I honestly couldn't believe it; manners were left in his van amongst his trash!

The staff came over and gave us a menu each, then asked if we wanted drinks. He still didn't put the bloody phone down. The more I looked at him, the more I saw how arrogant he was. After sitting around three to four minutes which did feel like thirty to forty minutes, he put the phone down and began calling the bar staff over like he was at the fucking Ritz.

Taking a deep breath in with a slow exhale out, I ordered a latte. Hurrying things up I quickly ordered from the menu feeling absolutely famished. I didn't want a starter, but he insisted we had one to share. The starter arrived about twenty minutes later and was positioned in the centre of the table. Suddenly, he was ramming the spiced king size prawns down my throat insisting I had to eat. Strange, I thought, I was the one who didn't want a starter. Being realistic, that was as romantic as the afternoon was going to be with him. There was absolutely zero chemistry.

During our main course, his phone was on the table and repeatedly ringing this mundane bloody tune. Between calls he'd have verbal diarrhoea, he couldn't shut up about this blonde female friend that he'd helped start up a business. Then how he didn't think this man or that man was right for her. 'Do you have a pic on your phone of her?' I asked. So, before his phone started to ring again, he showed me half a dozen pictures of her. This guy was either in love with this woman or badly infatuated with her, that's a definite observation. Straight out I asked him 'why are you here with me?' 'She won't date me,' he replied. 'She sees me just like a mate'. For fuck's sake not another love reject!

My patience has been tested once again!

A few minutes later his phone bellows, vibrating through the table. By the way, during the whole date he didn't bother to place it on silent either, his words: 'time means money'. Our main course had only started, so I politely requested he go outside to take the call, people were noticing his phone going off frequently.

Thankfully, I was left to finish my meal alone and in peace. He must have felt a tinge of guilt, as when he returned, he insisted I have a dessert, so cheesecake was ordered for two. While we were waiting, I zoned out while he still was waffling on about his own importance, repeatedly saying to me 'at the end of the day I'm a busy businessman'. I thought this guy must be on a repeat wind-up timer, nothing of interest is holding my attention. Waiting on dessert arriving, he goes back outside to take yet another call. That was my escape moment, I discreetly managed to text my daughter in law an SOS to come and rescue me.

Cheesecake was yummy, the plate scraped clean, and every bit of deliciousness was gone in a minute. I reached into my bag to grab my purse for my bank card, it was then he said to me the meal was on him. He didn't need to say that twice, thank fuck.

Looking at the situation another way, he'd had over an hour counselling session for free, when he wasn't taking a call! I should have been paid for enduring his shitty company and horrible demeanour. Since I do have manners and social graces, I thanked him for the meal and wished him all the best. Like a stuffed Christmas turkey, I waddled into the car park, where I spotted my daughter in law waiting for me. He hurried into his van and really floored it out of the car park, you'd have thought his arse was on fire. Never to be seen or heard from again, simply because Ms Blocker speedily blocked him.

Teeth Resembling Stonehenge

Time to touch base with my dating portal. On logging in I received another message from a guy who lived local to me. Joe seemed visually dowdy on his profile picture, however when we texted each other a few times he seemed likeable. After three days of texting, he asked me to go for a coffee or tea, positively I said yeah that's great. We both agreed to an introduction date in a local pub. My son took me there and waited with me in the car park.

Like the Christmas Boxing Day sales, an estate car arrived flying into the car park with some speed. My son and I sneered at each other both saying, 'that must be him'. Not a great first impression I thought, so let's see what he's like as he gets out of his car. I get out and wave bye to my personal taxi, while he slowly drives away watching me, as I'm watching him.

Joe gets out of his car and begins walking towards me with a closed smile, spontaneously he waves at my son, like he'd known him for years. My eyes tend to go very blurry quite often, and on this occasion, I could have done with my vision being fully blurred. As Joe approached me the penny dropped along with the look on my face. He began to smile wider as he got closer, I seriously took a double take. He displayed a mouth of what used to be teeth but now resembled Stonehenge. If you can imagine it was as if he had jaundice-coloured chiclets stuck randomly in parts of his gums, appearing in all different shapes and sizes and not all facing the same direction.

Now I'm not sure about you readers, but if you're anything like me, the appearance and importance of having teeth is a deal breaker. No wonder this man had no pictures of himself smiling, in fact I very much doubt he'd have had any luck on the dating scene exposing his empty mouth. Now don't go thinking I'm shallow, but there wasn't any way Joe was clinching a second date, I'd already made my mind up.

We sat at a corner table, he decided to sit sideways on his chair facing away from me, I sat against the wall side to support my back. Joe asked if I wanted a drink. 'Yeah, I'll have a cup of tea please,' I replied hesitantly. As he got up and went to the bar to order, I sneaked my phone from my bag and texted my son, 'please come back to get me'. 'Ok mam I'll be there soon', he replied.

Now this guy came back from the bar and mustn't have realised that I heard him order a pot of tea with two cups. What a stingy bastard sprung to mind. While waiting for the tea he was eagerly going on about changing jobs etc. I positively wanted to say fuck off, instead I had a couple of sips of tea then said, 'thanks for the cuppa but got to go, I've got a few things to do'. My son was waiting in the car park, as I sat down in his car, Joe got in his, waving and driving off like he'd done a hit and run. This guy seemed extremely highly strung to me. From beginning to end forty-five minutes in total and that dear reader is a first for me in record time. I just couldn't stop feeling repulsed at the presentation of his dirty mouth while he spoke or smiled.

I was sitting later that night, struggling to keep my eyes open, trying to watch something on Netflix. Then 'incoming' a ping … a text from

Joe. 'Erm you've not said anything so I will. I don't think there was any chemistry between us today, so there will be no second date'. Wow, no shit! I was astounded at the bloody audacity of him, I couldn't grasp his mentality of not being able to read the signs at all, surely, he must have known I had no interest in him from when I bailed out early. Why feel the need to have to send a text, unless he may have needed closure or was it control? I know I didn't. I'd rather kiss a toilet seat than speak to him again. Childish, yes, but true. Yuk!

One Pint of Urine a Day Keeps the Doctor Away

October 2019, and as usual a message landed via my online dating app. Why I attract the young bald or shaven-headed guys is beyond me especially since you readers all know I prefer hair. His message was pretty direct, 'Hey I like your pic and profile get in touch'. Apart from the bald head he had what I can only describe as a pretty-boy face, not a wrinkle in sight and very dark, defining eyebrows. His height around 5ft 10, not bad, his picture showed him outside posing playing a guitar. At first, I thought it could be a fake profile, but I wasn't totally sure as the pictures looked airbrushed to me.

I responded with my usual thank you for getting in touch reply and waited for what was next. 'Hey, my name is Aaron I'm from Corbridge, how about you?' The conversation continued back and forth for about an hour. To be honest at this point I think I was bored and flattered at the same time. I didn't really fancy him but was curious as to what he was after. Well yes, we all know what he was after, but I wanted to delve a little deeper. Find out if he had any substance to him!

He seemed friendly enough so far, so that when he asked for my WhatsApp number, I gave it to him. He didn't text, he sent voice messages. I wasn't comfortable with sending those, so I continued my replies with text.

'Hey, I'm Aaron, it's me again I'm just chilling in bed with Netflix, what you up to? Those replies on that dating site bloody hell I've got women wanting to hook up on first connection' he continued. 'Yeah, I get what you mean, so what you up to now?' I asked. Quickly he sent me a video call invite and a message saying he was free now, I hesitantly accepted.

There he was with a full naked hairy chest all on display while he lay back in bed smirking. I was taken back at his provocative presentation, but he remained pleasant while we briefly chatted. He was also older looking than on his pictures.

Our chat didn't last long as I wasn't comfortable chatting to him lying there naked in bed it felt wrong. What did evolve was the sudden enthusiasm of him recommending I drink my own urine twice daily as he'd been doing this for years. I tried not to look disgusted and said something like 'Oh right I must try it,' I didn't know what else to say! He then eagerly asked me to do some online research on the benefits of doing so. After our chat I did exactly that. I found absolutely no scientific evidence of this ritual being any good for you, which made me even more repulsed. Can you imagine his breath in the morning after drinking one warm cup of freshly squeezed piss!

A bit later on more voice messages landed. 'You're so lovely, it's ridiculous I'm incredibly happy but there's something I've got to tell you. I'm single because I have PTSD (Post Traumatic Stress Disorder). My step dad abused me into my twenties. It feels like I have bipolar because sometimes I need to be alone and sometimes, I want company. It's weird, I wish I were normal.'

94

'I had one girlfriend and all she wanted to do was to be dated, going out for meals etc. That's fine but all I want to do is chill at home and get a takeout. I wanted to share that with you.'

How the hell do I respond to that? I thought about it, so I disclosed I also have PTSD. It's something I've had for a long time and I'm not ashamed to say it's part of who I am and my survival through life. I then went on to say you are normal you just have different coping strategies than the average person. He then followed up with 'I believe everything happens for a reason and the stars are lined up for you and me, I'm so glad I called you ... I hope I've not put you off?' 'No, I like you you've not put me off' (I replied with gritted teeth, how could I say anything different after his disclosure).

As you can imagine he is saying mostly all the right things but I'm thinking you're running before you can walk with me mate. I'm not easily bowled over. Gut is rumbling with that warning feeling. Anyhow, I decided to see what he'd say to meeting for a coffee. 'Oh yeah, I can manage that as today you've made me feel great. I've had this depression for two days and it's starting to lift now.' When I have a good day, I'm really confident and sure of myself. I feel so fucking lonely tonight it's ridiculous I wish you were here to give you lots of cuddles as I feel like you're my girlfriend already.' What the fuck? It's laughable how some guys seem to think a few words involving girlfriend gets your knickers off. Not mine, my Bridget Jones belly warmers are staying firmly up!

It's utterly amazing how many men go on like this on a first chat. Sounds to me like it's another fanny rat on the loose.

Then he decides to say, 'I can't make Friday I'm freaking out thinking about it, I just want to see you, I'm so nervous, why am I so nervous?'

'How are we going to meet? Can I not support you go for a quiet coffee?' I asked. 'No, I'm not putting any further pressure on myself tonight I'm all over the place. We could go for a walk, or we could chill at yours or you could come to mine,' he replies. 'Aaron, I don't allow strangers to come to mine, nor me to theirs end of.' He responds, 'that's a shame because we both seem to really like each other. I feel you're my soul mate.' Then there was silence and a message popped up in the chat 'your security code with Aaron has changed. Tap to learn more'. This guy has more than one sim and is likely to be feeding the same verbal shit to multiple others.

'Have you changed your sim card Aaron?' 'No, the voice control thingy stopped working and I couldn't be arsed with it, so I restored the app.' Hmm I thought ... probable lie number one and counting!

'Do you ever get any time alone?' he asked. 'Yeah, my sons are always busy so plenty of me time.' 'Right well how about I drive over to yours tomorrow and we go for a walk around the block and once you know I'm not a mass murderer we can grab a drink in yours. If not, nice meeting you!' Wham bam thank you Ma'am springs to mind! I wonder what his reaction would be to my disability.

Ha-ha this guy is smooth, he knows what he's doing and the first thing he's using is his mental state to pull the empathy card into getting things done his way with no compromise. Now I'm just participating in chat to see how far he'll go. Not a hope in hell's chance of me meeting this guy.

'I'm free all night if you want to video call me as I actually miss your face, is that weird?' Treading gently, I said 'ha-ha no you must know what you like'. 'I feel alive around you,' he replied. 'Are you looking for a long-term relationship?' I asked. 'Yeah, I'm looking for a long-term relationship not to live with someone but to see my girlfriends two to three times per week. I used to live with someone, and she did everything for me, I lost my independence so I'm not doing that again.'

Two things that really jumped out at me. Firstly, he mentions girlfriend's plural, secondly, I could hear another phone text message in the background which confirmed he had two phones. Only one reason an unemployed guy would have with two phones and that's multiple hook ups going at the same time without the effort of dating. I think I should start my own company 'Sharon the Fanny Rat Hunter'. Has a ring to it pardon the pun!

'Do you have two phones, Aaron?' Immediately he became defensive. In my experience this is a glimpse of his guilt showing. If he has nothing to hide why become defensive. His response was 'I've only got one phone, if you think I'm hiding information from you and you're going to question everything I do or say then it's best we're just mates. I was with one girl, and she did this to me, she second guessed everything I told her which made me feel really anxious. That's no good to me.' Wow that was some speech! Very narcissistic I thought.

The conversation came to a halt after I said 'you really shouldn't class me as the same as your ex. To be fair I've not made assumptions I've reacted based on what I've heard. No way can I be put to the firing squad for being observant!'

The next morning a voice message arrived. 'Good morning my beautiful girlfriend, I've been for a lovely walk in the sunshine and tonight I'm going to Sunderland for drinks with one of my girl friends and I'm staying over at hers.' Apparently, he has mostly female friends of which are ex-girlfriends and whomever becomes his new girlfriend has to accept that. 'Have a great night out,' I said while thinking to myself he told me he can't even go out for a coffee... this guy has definitely got some game going on. At this point I grew a pair and told him that we'd make good friends only. The gentle let down approach.

What came back was 'please don't throw me away, I understand you've been hurt. We have a great connection, and you are my potential girlfriend.' What a crock of shit. This guy gets off doing this to females and I can assure you there will be a lot of women and possibly men with an axe to grind with this one!

He then blurts out 'I know we both want to rip each other's clothes off, but I know it's not just about that and I don't want to rush into a relationship with you.' Yesterday and this morning he felt like I was his girlfriend and now slow and steady wins the race. He certainly was right when he said his symptoms were likened to bipolar. This mind fuck was done in a few hours across two days imagine what this guy could do on a full-time basis. I'd be admitted to a psychiatric ward and locked in a padded cell. Good riddance!

Angela, Angela, It's Me!

Crisp white frosty mornings have arrived joined by the dark cosy winter nights of November. It's the time of year when I start planning and looking forward to Christmas. I looked on my dating profile to find there's a message from a guy who I thought looked very caring. It was a lovely close-up shot of him lying on his sofa with his little dog. Bob and I began to message each other back and forth. At this point I was neither here nor there in my opinion of him. He asked me out for lunch, and I thought hmmm he's not my type, but he may be a cracking person. On the plus side he's got a cute little dog so he should have a caring side.

The lunch date was planned for mid-November during the early afternoon. My Saviour my son, bless him, was able to drop me off again. It was another local country pub I'd chosen as a quick getaway if needed.

There was a sharp cold nip in the air and as soon as I arrived inside, I made a beeline for a warm seat beside the crackling log fire. While waiting for him, I drank a creamy hot latte, my phone rang, and it was Bob. 'Where are you?' he asked. I went on to describe where I was and ultimately, he'd gone to the wrong pub.

As I'm waiting cosy by the fire feeling extremely nervous, my throat becomes hoarser and drier. I slowly looked up finding myself being overshadowed by an extremely extra-large presence. His belly hung not too far in front of his thick knees. Although being a very tall man he struggled to put one foot in front of the other. I looked up then stood up to greet him, but already in my head I wanted to leave, I knew there was a zero chance of a relationship from my side. He offered to get me another latte as I'd just finished my first, just as they arrived at our cosy seats, we were moved into the restaurant area for our pre-booked lunch reservation.

We were sat at a tiny square table, I took one look and thought my fat arse will certainly struggle to squeeze in there, how the fuck his will I really don't know. Our starter arrived and while eating he told me he'd had a gastric bypass a few years back. Over the years he had found a cheeky way to cheat. This resulted in him putting most of his weight back on. You're not kidding, I thought to myself, he must have weighed around the twenty-five stone plus mark.

Yes, I know I've got my health issues, but I cannot be with someone who lives their life to eat, just no. There are usually more underlying issues that probably need resolving before he embarks on a relationship, at least that's what I thought. I've been through quite a bit of my own stuff; I need someone who's persona shines light and not a heavy burden for once.

While we were eating our main course he spontaneously decided to shout out to a lady while looking to his left. 'Angela, Angela, it's me'. This poor young lass looked startled, then looked at him puzzled. Finally, he finished cleaning his specs on his polo shirt and put them back on, then continued to blurt out 'shit I'm sorry, I thought you were Angela'. I just wanted to melt into a puddle. Why would anyone want to disturb someone eating their meal just because they think they know them? I was so embarrassed I didn't know where to look so I kept my head down as I ate my main course.

Dessert time and he asked me what I wanted. They had nothing interesting left on the set menu except ice cream so we both ordered that. During dessert he told me his wife had died of cancer a few years ago, but before she died, she racked up around £30k in debt. Unfortunately, he was responsible for gradually paying it off. That's not a great start for any new relationship at all, I thought to myself, lots of red flags. I've been there and I've done it, certainly not taking on anyone else's debt. The meal ended and I got out my purse to offer to pay my half. Without hesitation he marched me to the bar to pay my half of the bill, I'd noticed they put my second latte, the one he offered to pay for on my bill too, I didn't say anything just paid for it.

I went to the ladies' room, contemplating doing a runner, but I can't friggin walk without tripping over never mind run, so instead I texted my son to come pick up his mother who looked rather like a busted sausage at this point!

I returned to where the log fire was burning, and he'd bought coffees to my surprise. Sitting side by side in silence, he then leaned sideways and towards me, into my personal space. Attempting to be intimate, it seemed as if he were going in for a kiss, but then said, 'would you like to go out for another meal?' Just then my son texted: 'I'm outside Mam'. He could not have timed things better. I said to Bob I had to go, while walking towards the exit he shouted, 'I'll text you'. I sat in my sons car and said, 'quick drive, get me out of here please'.

We arrived home within fifteen minutes. There was a text immediately asking me out again. I took a step back while deciding on how to let him down gently. Before I replied another text came. 'Come on spit it out don't be a coward do you want to go out or what, just have the balls to tell me'. By now I was foaming at the mouth and had steam belting out my ears because of his rudeness. Eagerly I cracked on with my reply and I didn't hold back.

'How on earth can you expect to find a woman if you're inviting her for lunch and making her pay? If you cannot do a simple thing such as behaving like a gentleman and treating your date like she's important, then how are you going to get that respect back on future dates, I'm sorry we're not matched but wish you well', then hit my block button.

For those of you readers that think females should pay half on a first date that is fine, however I'm old fashioned I like the man to pay but I always offer. Usually that gives me an idea of what they are really like from the start. If there is a second date I pay, thereafter shared. I am set in my ways in that respect, and I don't think there is anything wrong with my way. I certainly know a few women that don't even bother to offer to pay and think the man should pay for everything.

The Fake Pylon Guy

It's the end of January 2020 and still no bae, boo, boyfriend, or other half, whatever you want to call it, absolutely zilch. I'm really starting to feel like I'm an undateable. Yes, I know my mobility isn't great and my weight, well let's face it, you look at me front ways on, and I'm not that wide. But look at me sideways and my huge fucking arse eclipses whatever lies around me. In fact, nothing about me seems to capture any man's attention these days.

I take another look at my online dating profile, and I read a pleasant message from a guy who lives near Trimdon Station. As we chatted Leo told me he'd been single a little while and would love to meet up for lunch or coffee whenever I wanted. His profile picture was smiley, so I knew he had teeth! Preferring a man to be of thicker build and he was of slim stature, but hey, I thought, don't judge.

After a day and night or two of chatting into the early hours Leo told me he had a last-minute booking at a local hotel called the Campanile. I was very sceptical when he told me he had his own business fixing pylon cables. Apparently, his team of lads were booked in there as completing work in the local area. 'Come over,' he said. 'I only want to hug you and get to know you'. Does this guy think he's dealing with a very naive stupid female here? I replied, 'tell you what, I won't come now because it's 3 am and not an appropriate time to meet you. How about I come over tomorrow?' 'Erm, yeah OK, what time?' he asked. 'Oh, erm, is 12 pm OK with you?' I replied. He then texted 'get a taxi over and I'll pay'.

A further hour of chatting continued, and he still tried relentlessly to get me to change my mind. Sticking my heels in I wasn't having any of it and said night, night. In the meantime, I did an online search for the Campanile Hotel, and as it happens, I'm familiar with where it is. While on the hotels website I checked out the facilities and most of all whether they had any lifts or not. They didn't to my surprise, so this made me feel a tad more on the secure side. You'll know why in a minute keep reading.

As the taxi approaches the reception area of the Campanile Hotel, a slim shadow of a figure inside the darkened doorway steps forward into the sunshine, cigarette hanging from his mouth. The scene reminded me of an old black and white detective film. I'd text ahead so I knew it would be him. He walked over to open the front passenger door to pay the driver as I got out. Then stood up and closed the car door, grabbed me for a hug and went in for a kiss on the lips. I quickly turned my face, where he plonked his lips on my right cheek. As he hugged me, he felt skeletal and crunchy like his bones were snapping. The appearance of his clothes resembled someone who may be homeless. Dressed in unwashed-looking denim jeans which were hanging off his what should be an arse, displaying his aged-looking underwear. Not a good look at all as he didn't even have an arse to put in those jeans. There was a few days' growth of blonde stubble on his face, and you could see he'd attempted to gel up his messy styled hair. Not sure what look he was going for, but it wasn't a good one. I could smell he'd smoked a joint, so his aroma wasn't resembling any cologne! Then to pop the cream on the top of the cake, he didn't look like his profile picture! Why am I not surprised?!!

He walked in front of me to open the door, manners I thought, one point scored. I followed him into what seemed like a hallway to rooms. 'Why are we in here?' I asked. 'We're going to my room,' he said. 'Why?' I asked. 'I've got coffee, tea or whatever you want in my room,' he said, at the same time he stood jingling his keys. 'Erm, where is your room?' I asked. 'It's on the second floor,' he replied. 'Where's the lift?' I asked, already knowing the hotel didn't have any. Secretly I would have shit myself if he said right over here. He looked directly at me, puzzled as he continued annoyingly to rattle those frigging keys.

'Well, we'll have to go into the reception area to see if we can get a drink there. The fact is I have poor knees and I can't climb stairs,' I said quite confidently. Do you know what he said? 'Climb on my back, hold tight and I'll give you a piggyback up to my room'. I'm a seventeen stone heifer and he's all of nine stone, I'd fucking paralyse him, I chuckled to myself. 'No, it's fine I'm good thanks', playing dumb. I knew only too well he wanted his leg over, but he wasn't getting it from me.

At the reception area he bought us refillable hot drinks. You couldn't even order a nice latte! There were a few people sitting having lunch at tables and not one time did he mention eating. Although in conversation he said he'd been out to the local shops in the morning to buy breakfast.

Collecting our drinks from the vending machine we sat on a ripped leather sofa where we began to chat about different subjects. The main topic he was banging on about was retiring and passing his business over to a manager. His forward planning was so he could have free leisure time to spend with me. Lots of me included in his future. Didn't believe a word, it's a tactic to get me into bed that's all.

I asked how long he was staying at the hotel, he said two nights due to work. The more I looked at him and the more he spoke it was clear to me he was a sex scammer, yes, another fanny rat. He was dodgy in every sense.

Now and again, he'd go outside for a smoke so the last time he did I called a taxi. My excuse there were things I needed to do. He went on to ask me to come down at night. I said, 'OK I'll try', but that was just to pacify him. I needed to get away safely, there was no way I was going back. My taxi showed up and he put a twenty-pound note in my hand to pay for it, which took me by surprise. My gut was off as this man clearly did not have a business but was a master of lies. Personally, I think he may be married and attempting to have a fling.

A few hours passed when I received a text from him asking if I was meeting him tonight. Sticking to my guns I replied no. No further texts followed. What can I say? He ghosted me! Never heard anything after that, then his profile disappeared from the dating site. All he wanted was sex, while telling lies and saying he wanted a relationship with me. Some men will push boundaries and they'll say what you want to hear to have no strings sex. That's fine if both consenting adults want that, but if one party doesn't the other should respect that in my opinion.

The Bag of Acid on a Train

End of March 2020 and social meetups regarding dating are out of the question for the moment, but I can still search and chat to people for the time being. I'd clicked like on a guy in my dating profile then he reciprocated by liking me back. A conversation began with him telling me he resided in the Teesside area, divorced with two kids, and looking for a relationship. I thought yeah, he's a tad younger than me let's see what his personality turns out to be like.

Izzy and I texted a fair bit first, then he asked me for FaceTime. I considered it and after I explained to him, I have anxiety he put me at ease.

FaceTime lasted for three hours, it felt comfortable appearing electronically in front of him. To my surprise we got on well until he mentioned my hair. He didn't really do anything wrong in his eyes but telling me that my hair was so noticeably thin was like putting a red flag to a bull.

Since I've had several health issues my hair has constantly fallen out. It's become too thin, resembling a hair sample you'd see on a hair chart in a hair salon. Years ago, my hair was my pride and joy, but now I'm ever so embarrassed about how little I have. Someone paying attention to how thin my hair looks certainly isn't a confidence builder!

Just wished my figure were the same, be fantastic to shed the pounds not the hair.

We still chatted for about a week, and he'd wanted to meet up soon. Mentioning that he was in the process of getting a car, but he didn't own one yet.

I couldn't blurt out I've mobility issues because I'd know he would strike me off, so I said, 'when you get your car you can come up to see me then'. Being face to face he could then judge me.

However, during one of the last conversations we had, I asked him if he'd ever been in prison. Not sure why, but my gut felt I needed to ask. 'Oh yeah that's why I'm not allowed a mortgage,' he said. My mind flipped, what a strange fucking thing to say! 'Why Izzy? What did you do?'. He grins, then laughs like a child doing some naughty antics. 'Tell me what happened, you can't keep me guessing,' I said. 'Well, I was travelling on a train down South, carrying acid in my bag. I left the bag accidentally behind on the train as I got off, and the acid leaked causing burning of the floor, while giving off poisonous fumes. People were evacuated'. He continues smoking a cigarette and smiling as he finishes his sentence saying he did time. 'Izzy, that is some crazy serious shit, it's like a terrorist attack,' I said straight out. That freaked me out because he didn't deny it, quickly my interest in him diminished. He wasn't fazed at all, like he didn't feel anything, that scared me!

In our very last conversation, he mentioned being intimate with me. My response was that I didn't know him yet. Then informing him it would take a few months before we got to that stage. His response was sorry, but I wouldn't wait months! Another 'fanny rat' for sure, he wanted sex without putting any effort into getting to know me. However, I had no intentions of anything becoming intimate. I learned that sometimes it's better to be diplomatic while backing away, especially when you find out they've done time!

That was the end of that. How fucking hard is it to find one genuine man that wants some real love and companionship? I'm becoming more and more exhausted by the whole thing it's exactly like digging for gold, I kid you not!

Mum Will Always Come First

I'm sitting in front of the TV, not finding anything that I wanted to watch, yeah you guessed I log onto my dating app on my phone. There's a message from a guy who I'd blocked last year, he must have made up another account. Richie and I engaged in conversation for over a week, this time around we'd accumulated around four hundred hours of FaceTime. The whole feel was much better between us, considering he apologised for his drunken silly behaviour that caused me to block him first time around. This time he assured me it wouldn't happen again. The sincerity of his apology made me start to like him a little bit more.

One night while we were chatting via FaceTime my phone screen suddenly turned white, then blank and silent. Then Richie appeared back on the screen. We carried on our chat and the same thing happened again within minutes. I thought it must be Wi-Fi issues on his side.

When he came back this time, I asked him what happened. He responded, 'My mum called me about something, then my friend so I put you on hold'. I was infuriated that he put me on hold twice, without saying excuse me or kiss my arse!

I previously mentioned there's one thing in a man that I insist he must have, and that's good manners. Richie's manners seem to have gone AWOL (absent without leave). I can't smooth it over and pretend nothing happened as being very facially expressive I can't hide my emotions. I asserted myself that night and refused to put my camera back on. He thought we were about to pick up where he paused me. 'What's wrong?' he said. I then went on to explain how rude he was curtly pausing me without a word, like it was acceptable or the norm. 'It's my mum and my friends and they will always come first,' he said. 'Crack on,' I replied, 'then keep doing that, see how many women will accept that sort of behaviour … Good luck', then blocked him for the second time.

I honestly was gutted at his response because we genuinely connected well. There was also a level of attraction between us that I've not experienced in years. To have to stand up for myself shouldn't be necessary but realistically I had to, he had to know I'm no pushover. If only he'd of handled the situation better, things would have not gone so pear-shaped.

To me he was exercising control over our situation. It felt like it was 'do as I say when I say' and that doesn't sit well with me. Over the years I've found many people like him, they confuse being controlling with being in control and that is so sad not knowing the difference. From day one I do tend to go in for the kill if I feel someone places me low down on their priority list. It's not a good feeling to have to constantly defend your personal value. I've battled this all my life not only with potential partners, but with family and friends too!

I've been through so much with shitty men my barriers and expectations have not budged since I began my online dating journey. I'm also at a point in my life since beginning to write my book that I'm starting to not give a shit about things that I used to. For example, if a man now commented negatively regarding my looks, I'd say something back that was sarcastic regarding his looks. Whereas up until not so long ago my sensitivity levels were so high, I'd easily be offended. Maybe it's an age thing or maybe it's an experience thing or it could be that I've used it as a form of therapy as when writing everything down things were made easier to process.

Groundhog Day

I'd not long woken up, mouth bone dry and feeling really parched. My tongue felt like coarse sandpaper, so I gulped a few mouthfuls of water. It was like being stranded in the Sahara Desert. As I finished rubbing my eyes to rid the blurriness, I checked my phone for the time. It wasn't midnight yet, but it felt like I'd been asleep for hours. Waiting for me was a text, Groundhog Day once again! Yes, you guessed, Ervin.

Checking my diary, it's been nine months since his last contact. My first thought ... at a loose end with no woman? What the fuck does this sewer rat want? Stay calm, I told myself, the more I'm polite the more inviting I'll be. He reads kindness for weakness and assumes too much so I have the upper hand. Knowing I'm never going back to him, it feels amazing to give him a taste of his own shit!

'How's you doing?' he asked in his pidgin English, 'I'm OK thanks'. 'Oh, I'm pleased you're safe,' he said, like he really meant it. The chat goes on, him saying that he was worried about me and with lockdown times are hard. Apparently, I've always been one of the kindest people he knows and wants me to reach out to him if I'm in any difficulties at all. That's me taken aback because never did I expect him to say that. However, it didn't stop there. 'I've been busy with my shops. I've got one opened and it's full and busy, so I'm opening another', he types.

Wow, this is a guy that was so tight with money, drove around in a £700 VW. Regularly taking on drug runs and now he's talking shops. Not sure if I buy into this again, he's a prolific liar and rotten to the core. The perfect example of a psychopath, narcissist, and a scammer.

He asks me where I'm living. I remind him of our chat the previous year and that jogged his memory. However, he still doesn't know where I live, he thinks I'm in Consett. In a nuisance type way, he asked for my number, obviously I refused and reminded him that he can use Messenger to call me free. 'I'm almost finished with work I will call you when I'm on my way home', he instructs me. Yeah, will you now, I said to myself. I snuggled back under my warm cosy duvet and comfortably went back to sleep with my phone still on silent.

On waking up again around 5.30 am I saw he'd rang and text via Messenger, so I text him saying I was asleep. That was my way of letting him know I'm not waiting around for him. To my surprise he replies, 'still awake can't sleep'. 'Have a Jack and coke that'll help relax you,' I said. 'No, I don't drink alcohol anymore, my life is good, I'm a changed, respectable man and I'm so happy for the first time in ages'. Then he proceeded to ask me if I'm still living in Gateshead. That's about three fucking times since he contacted me, and I've told him I live in Consett. What the fuck is this idiot on? At this point he thinks I'm two minutes away from where he now lives in Consett. I asked, 'what happened to the house you rented, in North Durham?', 'Oh I've sold it,' he replied. That's strange I thought, he'd told me he was renting it a few years back, the address is in one of my old diaries. Managing to source the information via the internet, it only just had gone up for sale.

I'm reluctant to accept things as the truth first-hand if I can research something I will. There are two options here, either he's lied about renting or he's possibly money laundering. The laundering he told me he was into back in 2012, where he decided in his home country to put his money into property. The other scenario could be he's managed to bleed dry vulnerable women over the years. He is the Devil himself and fortunately I'm lucky he got no money out of me!

Changing the subject: 'how are your daughters?'. I knew this would hit a nerve. 'I'm not allowed to see them, don't know where they are, and I don't want to talk about my past. My head is finally clear now and I'm in a happy place', he typed. 'Can I ask you something?' I just couldn't stop myself. 'When was your second daughter born?' '2013,' he said. 'So, you've clarified to me now twice that you cheated on me, as you and I were together from the summer of 2012,' I stated.

Then the real nasty piece of shit rears his head and starts with his gaslighting. That no longer works on me. 'What you are talking about, I'm a respected man and I only got in touch with you because you've been good to me in the past', blah bloody blah, as he furiously rambles on. Then as quick as snapping my fingers his mood lightened. He started reminiscing over how he'll never forget how good we were together, then asked to see me again. 'Yeah, I can see you as a friend no problem,' I said, knowing this would wind him up. Thinking, so fuck about time someone did.

Not liking that at all, he resorted to being filthy. Telling me what he was doing to himself at that moment. He then insisted on sending me a dick pic. 'Nah don't bother,' I said. Killing his moment, I asked what happened to his girlfriend. 'Doesn't work,' he replied and continued pushing for a naughty picture of me.

This will piss him off I thought, I sent him a decent one and yes with clothes on. It was about me being in control and not being controlled this time around. Lots of compliments, came wanting more pics, then I said, 'oh it's late I must sleep'. He continued saying please in several messages. 'No, no don't go yet please no, I'm begging I want a naughty pic. Come on it'll help me relax because I'm at work tomorrow night'. Who the hell does this guy think he is, asking me for naughty pics like it's the norm? I'm no angel but he can fuck right off. Finally, the ball landed in my court and after all these years it felt good, I slept intensely well that night. He didn't get any naughty pictures, how sweet revenge tasted!

Early afternoon came around and he'd text me asking what I was doing today. I knew he was on the verge of asking to meet up. He doesn't know I can't walk much so I just said, 'son and I spending time together and we're going on a walk'. 'Enjoy your walk,' he replies harshly, that seems abrupt I thought. Yeah, I spotted it, he starts to get furiously angry again. 'I don't need any woman for sex, I don't even think about it anymore. I've never been more fucking happy single, and I'll never let any fucker come into my life again'.

What the bloody hell just happened? He'd gone from playing with himself the night before, to wanting a naughty pic, then to a complete turnaround of remaining abstinent. It compared to dealing with two totally different people. I stayed calm and replied, 'stay safe and good luck with your shops'. 'I'm not at work tonight. I only work two nights a week,' he said. He'd previously told me he was at work tonight, once again more lies and games from a head player.

That for me is, and will be, the last time I'll ever give him my time, regardless. I have my personal closure after seven hurtful years, and I believe he realises now he can't get anywhere with me; he's spat out his dummy. That is my payback and a kind of personal reward.

On reflection, I really do think this monster has a lot of mental health issues that need to be addressed. Personally, I think he's extremely dangerous to society and this dear reader is why we all need to be cautious with online dating. You have got to learn how to separate the wheat from the chaff and that only comes with practice, don't let the scammers win and let it tarnish any hopes of you finding your best friend. I haven't, I'm still focused, but drained and weary, however still holding on to hope. I'm becoming better at spotting the fakes, scammers and Liars.

I'm on my ultra-last snoop regarding Ervin. First, I looked at his girlfriend's Facebook page, this time she had changed her status to single and removed all his pictures. Can you believe I was relieved that she had gotten wise to him? My gut told me to snoop a little more. Some further Facebook digging and what I found was just sickening to the core. Really this guy should be deported back to his own homeland for the number of females (and children's) lives he has potentially ruined. So don't think my comment has anything to do with racism. My point being he wouldn't be allowed in a strong Muslim Country to do what he's doing here, and rightly so!

There were pictures of him with another woman and a young baby possibly a boy, his first son. I looked at the dates posted of when the baby was born, and it really didn't take a genius to work it out. While she was pregnant, he was with his previous girlfriend. So, I wonder if he got caught out and she ended the engagement, then moved on to the new girlfriend with the baby. That makes perfect sense to me.

History repeats itself as it seems he's gone and done the same again to her, as he did to me back in 2012. Once a cheat is always a cheat in my experience. It's only just really hit me what a fucking lucky escape I have had. I'm now starting to regain my faith, believing that people are brought into your life for certain reasons, but also that your pathway is mapped out. If you see the warning signs of what pathway not to go down, stay focused and trust your gut. You see a red flag once, don't wait until there's twenty because that's already far too late. Time is precious to everyone but with these leeches it's a head game, they thrive on our vulnerability, and they love drama. Nothing is their fault, but everything is ours!

Guess Whose Face Showed Up?

The UK was the first in the World reported to begin the vaccination programme in December 2020 and statistics showed that they were on target for the speed of delivering the programme. At last, this offers a bit of hope for the new year ahead, an insight of normality on its way for everyone.

Whilst talking about technology, instead of the usual dating app I used, I decided to use the newly launched social media one, thinking my luck may be better trying something different. Looking at things with a fresh approach and all that jazz! Not to forget it was linked to my social media account, if I did match with anyone, I could add them on Messenger and do a bit of my inspector snoop. Plus, I did think there would be less scammers. How wrong could I be! Unfortunately, many are still going strong with their fake profiles.

I'm clicking on a heart symbol which indicates a like and lets the other person know. I don't mind doing this bit to get a match, but I'm not the type that usually initiates chat. My phone is in my hand and I'm sitting browsing the minuscule choices that are brought my way. So far, I'm not impressed, if anything it's one of those for fuck's sake moments when I just don't know if I should laugh or cry, but I persevere!

My TV is on with Netflix playing *Making a Murderer* in the

background. Don't ask me why I'm watching this kind of stuff, scaring my tits off as I'm sat in the dark by myself. Even my cats aren't anywhere to be seen. Then guess whose face showed up clicking on a heart for me. You know that feeling you get when you're taken by surprise in a nice way. Your heart jumps and you get a weird feeling in your gut but not a warning feeling. Richie the guy who put me on hold during his two calls! I'm wondering why after six months he has gotten back in touch, or did he not recognise me? I'm always suspicious and cautious.

I girlishly giggle as I click on a return heart, I know I'm a nosy cow but I'm curious to know if he remembers me. Within three minutes of me returning a heart there's a message. 'Hi sweetheart how have you been, you beautiful woman?'. I replied saying, 'ah you do remember me, I thought you'd made a mistake'. 'A mistake, no way. You blocked me last year, so I've been searching for you since, I did make another profile up and contacted you the other month, but you didn't respond'. 'Yes, I know but when I saw you trying again this time, I thought I'd see how you were.'

I'm keeping it very cool by the way, but at the same time elated at how he's tried to find me these last few months. It's lovely to feel like I'm wanted, let's face it, we all want that feeling, it's human nature. That doesn't make me weak though! My barriers remain in place guarding my emotions as I'm not easily sucked in. Like most people, I'm ready to be loved and not played head games with.

After about half an hour of chat he firmly asks for FaceTime with me. When we linked up before and he did what he did to me I agreed but with terms. 'Yes, you can see me but if you get a call don't be rude putting me on hold, this time I won't be waiting for you on your return'. 'No, no, no, I'm so deeply sorry that will never happen again. I was so stupid, I can't do that to you anymore,' he replies. Bloody hell, this is a turnaround, I think to myself, but if something is too good to be true it usually is.

We began to FaceTime, and we hit it off like a house on fire. A few hours into the night, after enjoying a good laugh tinged with a bit of harmless flirtation, he said to me 'Sharon listen, I don't want you to block me again. Teach me, talk to me, if we have a problem, we can sort it out like adults. I really, really more than like you, I'd like it if you'd consider to be my girlfriend. I've not felt like this in ages, and I knew when we first met you were different. I know we're living in difficult times, and this has made me realise what I want, and this is you, don't break my heart!'.

Taking a few minutes in silence to digest his words I then replied, 'these are not normal circumstances and while we can only communicate via FaceTime, I'm also not interested in multi chatting. I also refuse to get into anything naughty online, to me that is just tacky and cheap, especially since we have not met in person. However, I do feel like we complement each other very well. On that note I would like us both to exclusively chat to each other and if that terminology of 'girlfriend-boyfriend' cements that for you I'll agree. However, that doesn't give you exclusive entry into my lady garden if you understand. We really need to know each other for a few months before we embark on taking it to the next level'. He understood then agreed, the serious chat ended on a light and fluffy note, with us moving over to chatting more on WhatsApp.

Over the week we'd chatted several times during the day and night via FaceTime. This was in between his job as a taxi driver. In that time, he kept wanting to come and pick me up to go for a ride or have something to eat at my house or his. I've never in my life randomly opened my home to any man ever or gone back to theirs. Decisively I kept refusing his requests, it's not my idea of getting to know someone. I need to be dated, courted the old-fashioned way, and not coerced into anything I'm not comfortable with. I've mentioned before how vulnerable I feel with my illness and in no way am I placing myself into what could be a dangerous situation. Not to mention it's a fucking pandemic and he wants to break the rules, but there's no way I am.

'I'm a taxi driver don't worry; you won't get fined I'll get out of it easy'. A few times he repeats this and I'm getting a bit fed up with hearing it. I refuse him again, saying I have my priorities and my principles simple. What's the hurry? I'm thinking, but there can only be one reason, sex!

Saturday evening and we're chatting via text on WhatsApp. I asked him to add me on Messenger so I could send him some funny gifs. It was also a little excuse to snoop on his Facebook. While on his Facebook page, I scroll through the bits he's allowed publicly. Nothing jumps out regarding any women or relationships and his status is displayed as single.

My phone pings letting me know I've received a notification. Richie started following me because I didn't add him as a friend. Following, hmmm I thought to myself, while I'm in such a curious phase I decided to look at who he is following. This section was on view, fully accessible to anyone too. I found he was following at least one hundred people. Single mams accounted for seventy-five per cent, ranging from student age to mid-forties all living in the same area as himself … interesting!

I was the last added onto his following list which was great. It would be a good comparison guideline to use to see if he's chatting or still searching for a female, after he's become exclusive to me. My thoughts were why does a man in his late forties have student age females on his Facebook? I'm sure you'd all agree in thinking that it's a tad weird, it made me cringe but also curious.

That following afternoon we'd been speaking as usual. At that point I didn't see any reason to bring up the subject of whom he's following. Until a bit later when I decided to snoop and check his followers. To be honest there had only been a few hours gone by, so I didn't expect to see anything different. Fuck! How wrong was I ... thanks to my gut feeling I snooped.

He'd added another single mother who lived near him, she was roughly in her mid-twenties. I screenshot the evidence in case he decided to make private his following section and deny it. My intention was naturally to ask him about it. Yes, you readers could argue if he had anything to hide why didn't he make whom he follows private? What I could not get my head around was why did he want me to be exclusive to him? Why search for me? Why after only hours of following me, did he add that female if he had no intentions with her? Nah, I hold in my hand a big friggin red flag. Therefore, I'm suspicious, and it's probably why I'm still single. Trust has got to be earned in my opinion.

When questioned he said he couldn't remember adding her. Then he remembered and thought the previous week. He went on to justify he'd not spoken to her or any female since talking to me. Then the gaslighting showed up. 'You have followers on your Facebook'. 'Yes, I do,' I replied, 'but there is a huge difference between following females as you do. I follow businesses not men specifically!' He wasn't having any of it, as he'd not lied or done anything wrong in his mind. To me he'd overstepped that mark. Imagine if it was me following a new man? I'm sure that wouldn't sit well. He repeatedly continued to tell me he's a good man, he doesn't cheat or lie! Yeah right, those that try and convince you that they are the best thing since frozen diced onion, are the ones to doubt! Pinocchio is a real person too and he doesn't lie either!

He ended up blocking me, that shows me he must feel guilty. So much for talking like adults. How far he pushed my boundaries to get into my knickers, it's crazy when I think about it. Why can't people be happy with what they have instead of wanting more? Really pisses me off big time!

You Couldn't Write It Could You?

'Pas de regrets' as they say in France or in the Queen's English 'no regrets'. After all these years during my online dating search I'm still presently single, same as I was when I started back in 2012. My journey has taught me the hard way on many occasions. Teaching me that any regrets are futile because they fester as they bury deep in your soul, they try to destroy you. Don't hoard those feelings like I once did, they are non-productive. Let them go, shake them off because tomorrow is a new day, and it isn't guaranteed!

How exhausted I feel doesn't even cover where my emotions are at right now. It's been several years since I started to consciously search for one 'spare' good man. Up until now my experiences have produced the dregs of male society. A few of them from different cultures and backgrounds too, I don't discriminate. Then when I've analysed my dates no fucking wonder most are single, they could do with being taught how to treat and love a woman honestly.

For you readers who have been ghosted don't waste your time waiting for closure like I did, that time may never come. Unfortunately for me, finding closure took several years out of my life. It took a lot of my patience and energy to see it through and I won't get my life or that time back. Now it's done and it is what it is. I'm moving forward with tiny steps in the hope of making huge progress! If you find yourself joining the online dating crowd my advice would be to tread carefully. Using caution to move on but not forgetting to listen to your gut.

On reflection, this whole lockdown situation has got to have changed the way people value people. Rumours are going around saying it's all part of a 'New World Order'. Whether it is or isn't, we must live the best possible lives we can because just like this pandemic we don't know what could happen next. Regardless of all the conspiracy theories out there, instead of worrying myself utterly sick like I used to, I try to research a little out of curiosity, then put it to the back of my mind. Let's face it, if there are Aliens walking amongst us, what can we do? We've come too no harm so far.

Now I recall several occasions with Mary, with whom I'd shared some of my darkest experiences in life. On one occasion she was in so much disbelief, she followed up by shaking her head then saying with a smile 'Sharon, you couldn't write it could you'. The irony was that I thought yeah, I can, why not share the hard and comical times I've had? It's made me the strong woman I am today. Sadly, I wish she'd have lived long enough to read my online dating memoirs.

Concluding, my dear readers, please don't forget to enjoy what beauty in life you have around you. Appreciate your family and friends, don't take them for granted. Never make a 'nothing' into a 'something', it's not worth missing out on valuable human time together. Live for today and leave the past behind, but most of all stay safe while living with our biggest invisible enemy Covid-19 …

Sharon J Reah, 2021.